TWAYNE'S WORLD AUTHORS SERIES

A Survey of the World's Literature

Sylvia Bowman, Indiana University

GENERAL EDITOR

GERMANY

Ulrich Weisstein, Indiana University

EDITOR

Karl Marx

(TWAS 296)

TWAYNE'S WORLD AUTHORS SERIES (TWAS)

The purpose of TWAS is to survey the major writers —novelists, dramatists, historians, poets, philosophers, and critics—of the nations of the world. Among the national literatures covered are those of Australia, Canada, China, Eastern Europe, France, Germany, Greece, India, Italy, Japan, Latin America, the Netherlands, New Zealand, Poland, Russia, Scandinavia, Spain, and the African nations, as well as Hebrew, Yiddish, and Latin Classical literatures. This survey is complemented by Twayne's United States Authors Series and English Authors Series.

The intent of each volume in these series is to present a critical-analytical study of the works of the writer; to include biographical and historical material that may be necessary for understanding, appreciation, and critical appraisal of the writer and to present all material in clear, concise English—but not to vitiate the scholarly content of the work by doing so.

Karl Marx

By JULIUS SMULKSTYS

Indiana University, Fort Wayne

Twayne Publishers, Inc. :: New York

Library of Congress Cataloging in Publication Data

Smulkstys, Julius.
  Karl Marx.

  (Twayne's world authors series, TWAS 296. Germany)
  Bibliography: p.
  1. Marx, Karl, 1818–1883.
HX39.5.S56   193   73–17398
ISBN 0–8057–2595–4

Preface

As is well known, Karl Marx was one of the most prolific and far-ranging writers of modern times. He authored numerous books, studies, pamphlets, essays, and articles which established him as a philosopher, historian, economist, sociologist, political scientist and, above all, as a social critic. Marx also wrote poems, one play, several literary critiques, and started to work on a major study of art history. Since these efforts were outside the mainstream of his intellectual interests and qualitatively and quantitatively represented only marginal accomplishments, they failed to establish him as a poet, playwright, literary critic, or art historian. Yet, despite the limited value of these literary writings, they cannot be dismissed as irrelevant to his major intellectual pursuits.

One of Marx's lifelong objectives was the redefinition of man's purpose and role in the world. In order to explain man in terms of the totality of his experience, potentials, aspirations, and future prospects, he developed many concepts of man relating to his social, economic, political, religious aspects, each denoting a different human dimension. As far as the concept of the literary and artistic man was concerned, Marx left only scattered utterances and hints that suggest rather feeble attempts to elaborate on one human dimension in the process of rounding out the total concept of man. But whatever the intrinsic merits of his pronouncements on literature, they constitute an integral part of his system of ideas and, therefore, cannot be fully appreciated outside its conceptual framework. For this reason, the first four chapters of this study are devoted to Marx's philosophical, economic, and political views. Chapters Five, Six, and Seven focus on his theory of literature, literary critiques, and on his style. The last chapter also indulges in the discussion of Marx's youthful poetry and play-writing, achievements that made no identifiable impact on contemporary literature and are interesting largely for the occasional insights into his complex personality and into the possible motives underlying some of his subsequent ideological commitments and political actions.

Marx's principal ideas were developed around a set of assumptions which, through successive phases of his life, evolved into a system of parts that more or less fit into a larger whole. More or less, because the system contains a greater amount of contradictory, irrelevant, or ambiguous theories, concepts, and terms than is usually the case in such grandiose designs. In Marx's world of ideas, the dichotomies of system and chaos, logic and inconsistency, precision and ambiguity abound. This partially explains why his doctrines lend themselves so easily to contradictory interpretations. Questions such as whether there was one or two Marxes in terms of the evolution of his thought, or whether he did, or did not, consider revolution as inevitable in the proletarian struggle for power have been the objects of many heated debates among scholars, official guardians of the true faith, revisionists, and anybody who has found the many vicissitudes in the development of the Marxist dogma to be a fascinating subject.

The purpose and the scope of this book, however, ruled out a more comprehensive discussion of Marx's fundamental theories and their assessment by prominent students of Marxism. The chapters on the development and substance of his thought are primarily intended to provide an adequate theoretical background for a thorough evaluation of his literary contributions. The chapter on revolutionary activism has a similar objective in focusing on Marx's efforts to reconcile the imperatives of theory and practice, a problem that stalked him throughout his entire life and once more reappeared in the form of discrepancies between his theory of literature and his personal literary preferences.

Marx and Engels repeatedly asserted that there were no theoretical or tactical differences between their views. The available evidence tends to support this claim: in addition to collaborating in the writing of numerous major works, they closely cooperated on virtually all works that were individually written. Perhaps even more significantly, their voluminous private correspondence as well as reminiscences recorded by their relatives, friends, and followers fail to disclose any important disagreements. But differences of emphasis, nuance, and predilection for certain subjects obviously existed. For example, Engel's studies in the natural sciences and in anthropology, for the most part undertaken after Marx's death, opened new dimensions in Marxism. Whether Marx would have endorsed them is impossible to say, but there is little doubt that the studies were intended to enrich, not modify, the body of thought formulated while the senior member of the team was still alive. Because much of what Marx and Engels wrote was complimentary in terms of elaboration, simplification, or introduction of subjects ignored by the other, Engel's writings will be occasionally cited in order to reinforce or explain my interpretations of Marx's views and actions.

The quotations from Marx's and Engels's works are taken from the standard English translations listed in the bibliography. Since their collected works have not yet been published in English, I had to depend on a variety of sources of uneven quality. In general, the more recent translations issued in the United States and Great Britain are of superior quality both in terms of style and accurate reflection of the authors' intent. On the other hand, the older translations issued in the Soviet Union or subsequently reissued in the United States under private auspices are definitely inferior on both counts. Wherever it was possible, I tried to use the more recent American and British versions. In some cases, however, the use of the older versions was unavoidable. Moreover, since some works of Marx and Engels were translated in installments by different translators and published by different publishers at different times, in several instances quotations from the same work had to be taken from two or three different sources.

I want to express my gratitude to the many institutions and individuals who helped me in writing this book. Special thanks goes to Indiana University which supported the project in the form of two summer grants and a sabbatical leave; to Mr. Fred Reynolds, Director of the Fort Wayne Public Library, who generously put the research facilities of his library at my disposal; to Miss Janet Smith whose work on the grammar and the syntax of the text was invaluable; to my colleagues at the Fort Wayne Campus of Indiana University whose suggestions contributed more to the success of the project than they probably realize; and, above all, to my family who stoically endured all the hardships and frustrations associated with this undertaking.

JULIUS SMULKSTYS

March, 1973
Fort Wayne, Indiana

Contents

Chronology

1818   On May 5, Karl Marx is born in Trier, Prussia, to Heinrich Marx and his wife, the former Henrietta Pressburger.

1830–   Attends Gymnasium in Trier.
1835

1835   Enters law school at the University of Bonn.

1836–   Transfers to the University of Berlin; studies law, philoso-
1841   phy, and history.

1837   Joins the Young Hegelians; begins an intensive study of Hegel.

1838   Father dies.

1841   Receives Ph.D. from the University of Jena.

1841–   Contributes to and eventually becomes the editor of the
1842   liberal *Rheinische Zeitung* (Rhenish Gazette).

1842   Meets Friedrich Engels.

1843   Under pressure from the state censor, he resigns as editor of *Rheinische Zeitung*; marries Jenny von Westphalen; works on *Kritik des Hegelschen Staatsrechts* (Critique of Hegel's Philosophy of the State); moves to Paris; writes *Zur Judenfrage* (On the Jewish Question) and *Zur Kritik der Hegelschen Rechtsphilosophie: Einleitung* (Toward the Critique of Hegel's Philosophy of Law: Introduction).

1844   With Arnold Ruge he publishes the *Deutsch-französische Jahrbücher* (German-French Annals); studies political economy, socialism, French history. His daughter Jenny is born; he writes *Ökonomisch-philosophische Manuskripte, 1844* (Economic and Philosophic Manuscripts of 1844); begins a lifelong friendship and collaboration with Engels, with whom he writes *Die heilige Familie oder Kritik der kritischen Kritik* (The Holy Family or Critique of Critical Critique).

1845   Leaves Paris for Brussels under orders of the French government; writes *These über Feuerbach* (Theses on Feuerbach); his daughter Laura is born.

1845– Collaborates with Engels on a second major work, *Die*
1846 *deutsche Ideologie* (The German Ideology).

1846 His son Edgar is born.

1846– Writes *Misère de la Philosophie* (The Poverty of Philoso-
1847 phy), originally written in French.

1847 Joins the Communist League; the League's Second Congress instructs Marx and Engels to draft its program.

1847– With Engels he writes *Manifest der kommunistischen*
1848 *Partei* (The Communist Manifesto).

1848 Arrested and expelled from Belgium; returns to Germany via Paris and takes an active role in the revolution; becomes editor of the radical-democratic *Neue Rheinische Zeitung* (New Rhenish Gazette).

1849 Acquitted by a jury in a trial resulting from charges of sedition. Expelled from Prussia, he settles down in London to begin an exile which lasts until the end of his life. His son Guido is born.

1850 Collaborates with Engels on *Ansprache der Zentral behörde an den Bund* (Address of the Central Committee to the Communist League); writes *Die Klassenkämpfe in Frankreich, 1848–50* (The Class Struggles in France, 1848–50); temporarily associates with Blanquists; resumes economic studies; Guido dies.

1851 His daughter Franziska is born. He begins a decade of article writing for *The New York Tribune*.

1851– Writes *Der Achtzehnte Brumaire des Louis Bonaparte*
1852 (The Eighteenth Brumaire of Louis Bonaparte).

1852 Franziska dies. He dissolves the Communist League.

1855 His daughter Eleanor is born; Edgar dies.

1857– Prepares manuscripts on criticism of political economy,
1858 posthumously published as *Grundrisse der Kritik der politischen Ökonomie* (Fundamentals of the Critique of Political Economy).

1858– Writes *Zur Kritik der politischen Ökonomie* (A Contribu-
1859 tion to the Critique of Political Economy).

1860 Writes *Herr Vogt* (Mr. Vogt).

1862– Writes *Theorien über den Mehrwert* (Theories of Surplus
1863 Value).

Chronology

1863	His mother dies.

1863   His mother dies.
1864   Helps found the Working Men's International Association; drafts the Association's *Inaugural Address* and *Rules*, both originally written in English.
1864–   Plays a leading role in the General Council of the Working
1871   Men's International Association.
1867   Publishes the first volume of *Das Kapital* (Capital).
1867–   Works on the second and third volumes of *Das Kapital*.
1880
1871   Writes (in English) *The Civil War in France*.
1872   Instigates the transfer of the General Council of the Working Men's International Association to New York.
1875   Writes *Randglossen zum Gothaer Partei Programm* (Critique of the Gotha Program).
1879   With Engels he writes a letter attacking socialist revisionism.
1879–   His health begins to deteriorate.
1883
1881   His wife dies.
1883   Marx and his daughter Jenny die.
1895   Engels dies.

CHAPTER 1

The Humanist

KARL MARX was born on May 5, 1818, in Trier, a provincial town in the Palatinate. Although there was a long line of rabbis on both sides of the family, six years after his son's birth the elder Marx, in order to avoid the recently adopted anti-Semitic laws, had the entire family converted in the Prussian Evangelical Church. At the age of seventeen, Karl was sent to the University of Bonn to study law. The evidence is somewhat fragmentary but it appears that he had a tumultuous social life there and totally neglected his studies. A year later, the father, alarmed by his son's frivolous activities, including a duel and an arrest for illegal possession of firearms, transferred Karl to the more sedate and intellectual atmosphere of the University of Berlin.

I *The Disciple of Hegel*

Berlin, at that time, was the center of Hegelianism, with which the young student inevitably came into contact. He regularly attended Eduard Gans's lectures on jurisprudence and was greatly impressed by the professor's application of the Hegelian method to the systematic and critical study of legal institutions. Once Karl Marx became interested in Hegel, he decided to read all of the old master's works, emerging from the ordeal a confirmed Hegelian. Subsequently, he abandoned law for philosophy and history and wrote a doctoral dissertation on the differences between the Democritian and Epicurean philosophies. In the true Hegelian spirit, young Marx argued that Epicurus was the more advanced philosopher because he succeeded in solving dialectically the contradictions found in the materialism of Democritus. In 1841 Marx was awarded the degree of Doctor of Philosophy from the University of Jena.

Hegel, one of the most influential post-Kantian philosophers, distinguishes between a spiritual world that is real and a phenomenal world that is apparent. Human experience begins with imperfect knowledge obtained through the senses. Gradually man advances to higher forms of understanding which culminate in the truth of reason, or knowledge of the world as revealed by philosophy. At first, the subject and the object seem to be separated and hostile to each other. But the advance of knowledge shows that this is not so. The object can be fully known only as a part of the subject. In order to understand the individual object, man has to go beyond it into the realm of thought, which is more general, inclusive, and therefore more real. Thus the reality of the object is absorbed in the mind. Or, putting it differently, the real object is created by the intellectual activity of the subject.

Hegel identifies the development of self-consciousness with mankind's progress toward freedom. Self-consciousness becomes simultaneously epistemological and historical process, in which successive forms of consciousness appear as various stages of history. Since Hegel was disillusioned with contemporary politics, especially as exemplified in the destructiveness of the French Revolution, he maintains that the subject's true freedom can be realized only in the realm of the mind. Specifically, through the knowledge of dialectical philosophy the subject becomes aware of itself as an object; or, man becomes truly free because he knows and possesses the world as his own reality. The world is now the fulfillment of man's self-consciousness. The totality of self-consciousness, or spirit, which comprehends all thought and experience according to an ideal logical system, is called the Absolute. World history is the dialectical unfolding of the Absolute as a concrete idea, or the development of the ubiquitous spirit as an entity becoming aware of itself.

One of the key elements in the Hegelian system is the dialectic. It purports to explain change in the spiritual as well as the phenomenal world. The Greeks used this term to describe a discussion in which two participants start with diametrically opposed views, later modify them by accepting parts of the other's position, and eventually adopt a broader view that does justice to both original stands.

Hegel believes that the thought process, and therefore all reality, is governed by the dialectical pattern; it begins with the assertion of something positive, a thesis, which is negated by its opposite, or antithesis, and subsequently results in the resolution of the contradiction, or synthesis. The synthesis, in turn, produces its own negation, and the same triadic pattern is repeated many times over until it yields a synthesis without inherent contradiction. To Hegel the dialectic is not an exercise in formal logic, but the reflection of progress in the life of an idea. The "last" synthesis represents the final stage in the idea's self-development from an abstract to a concrete concept, or the Absolute. Since nature and history are regarded by Hegel as mere reflections of the Absolute Idea, he applies the dialectic to interpret both.

There are three laws, or stages, of the dialectic. *The law of the transformation of quantity into quality* asserts that any substantive (qualitative) change in thought, nature, or history is preceded by the accumulation of hardly detectable minor (quantitative) changes. At a certain point—Hegel calls it *node*—the cumulative effect of the quantitative changes suddenly causes a transformation in quality. For example, the constant application of heat to water will at first produce only an increasing number of bubbles, but at 100° Centigrade water will begin to turn into steam. One of the important corollaries of this law is the claim by some contemporary Marxists that all qualitative changes occur suddenly as if by leaps.

The law of the union of opposites consists of two assertions: (1) that reality is essentially contradictory, and (2) that the contradictions exist in union with each other. Good and evil are opposites, but one cannot understand the one without understanding the other. Likewise, the notion of darkness cannot be appreciated without the notion of lightness. To use still another example, a road to the east is also a road to the west if viewed from the opposite direction.

The law of the negation of the negation proclaims that the driving force behind the dialectical process is the dynamic power of the negative. Although the contradictions exist in union, they are not permanently united. Sooner or later the balance shifts and one of the components assumes a dominant position toward its opposite. Change occurs when, having reached the node, the thesis (one component in the union of contradictions) is negated by its antithesis (the other component). This phase represents an effort, dynamically arising from the friction produced by the opposites, to remove the contradictions of the thesis. The antithesis inevitably develops its own contradictions, however, and the same process is repeated. One component of the second union becomes dominant and negates its opposite (negation of the negation). The result is the third, highest union—Hegel calls it synthesis—which incorporates entirely new elements as well as valid parts of the original thesis and antithesis. The synthesis is, of course, just another thesis that again experiences double negation.

A tyrannical government and a freedom-loving but oppressed people can be said to represent two opposites forming a thesis. Through the revolutionary process, a node is reached that signifies the overthrow of tyranny and the introduction of anarchy, a condition without government. But anarchy, the antithesis of the negated thesis, is also oppressive because absence of government means that no effective force exists to protect an individual's freedom from infringements by other persons. Thus evolves a new contradiction (freedom-loving people versus anarchy) and a new negation, resulting in the reintroduction of government—but with constitutional safeguards to protect the rights of the people.

Hegel's philosophy can be summarized as follows:

(1) It postulates the primacy of the ideal, or the spiritual, relegating the material to passivity and dependence on the ideal.

(2) It assumes that history is a rational process governed by the laws of the dialectic.

(3) It presupposes that truth and reality lie in the complete whole. For example, the rationality of isolated historical events is determined by their contribution to and participation in the unfolding of the ultimate reality and truth, the Absolute.

(4) It is essentially an optimistic philosophy. Hegel regards the world as a dynamic and spiritual process that advances toward a rational order. What occurs last is qualitatively more complete and therefore more real and rational.

II   The Young Hegelian

In Berlin Marx joined the Young Hegelians, also known as the Hegelian Left, whose professed attachment to Hegelianism did not prevent them from modifying the old master's philosophy to suit their own temperament and views on contemporary religious and social questions. Apart from their fascination with Hegelianism, the one common denominator that bound this diverse group of individualists was their passionate opposition to all established religions, political institutions, and social systems.

[18]

The Young Hegelians emphasized the distinction between Hegel's reactionary system and his revolutionary dialectical method. The latter, presupposing a continuous change out of logical necessity, fit very well into the young radicals' plans to change the existing order. On the other hand, it is hardly surprising that they were distinctly cool to the system built around the Absolute Spirit, whose ultimate political realization was to be found in the Prussian monarchy.

The Young Hegelians began their attack on the Establishment with a critique of institutionalized religion. David Strauss, author of *The Life of Jesus (Das Leben Jesu)* whose publication in 1835 produced instant shock waves throughout Germany, characterized the Gospels as a collection of myths that originated in the early Christian communities and saw Spirit in the communal consciousness or mind. Bruno Bauer, one of Marx's closest friends at the University of Berlin, declared Christianity to be an invention of unscrupulous persons with ulterior motives, and identified Spirit with individual consciousness. Ludwig Feuerbach, the critic of Hegel who had the greatest impact on the young Marx, explained religion in terms of various human needs.

Feuerbach's principal complaint is that Hegel inverts the relationship between subject and predicate, or thought and being, or God and man. Man is not, as Hegel insists, the expression or predicate of the divine thought process. On the contrary, the divine thought process is the attribute of man, the subject. The true reality is to be found in the individual human being; and Hegel's Absolute Spirit is merely a man-made illusion.

Feuerbach's interpretation of religion parallels his critique of Hegel. He maintains that man created God after his own image in order to satisfy his psychological needs. Man attributes to God ideal human characteristics that he himself cannot realize because of adverse material conditions. Thus, God becomes the image of what an individual would like to be but is not: the possessor of absolute knowledge, infinite love, supreme wisdom, and so forth. In this manner, man views God as a separate object, as something alien to himself.

Feuerbach's notion of religious alienation approximates Hegel's idea of alienated spirit, which experiences the external world as a separate and hostile entity in its progress toward self-consciousness. Moreover, in religion as in speculative philosophy, the attributes of man are transformed into abstract subjects. Consequently, Feuerbach maintains that in order to reveal the true nature of philosophy and religion, the attributes of man have to be restored to their proper status as predicates and man to his proper status as a subject.

The starting point of Feuerbach's philosophy is not an abstract concept conceived in the mind of a philosopher, but man and his actual experience. Although he assumes that the principal forces in the historical process are material rather than spiritual, in his respect for ideas, his notion of alienation (though an "inverted" one), and his frequent use of the dialectic, Feuerbach remains essentially a Hegelian.

III Acquaintance with Socialism

After graduation Karl Marx planned to pursue an academic career, but his close association with the Hegelian Left ruled out job possibilities at a German university. Thus, when in October, 1842, an opportunity arose to edit a recently formed newspaper, he immediately seized upon it. Originally, the *Rheinische Zeitung* was intended to be a middle-class organ that would reflect the provincial interests of the Rhineland and not necessarily be antagonistic to the ruling Prussian monarchy. The organizers of the editorial board, however, happened to be sympathetic to the philosophical and social ideas of the Hegelian radicals and proceeded to recruit editors and contributors from this group. During Marx's editorship, the *Rheinische Zeitung* became an effective instrument of social criticism and seemed to be well on the way to developing into the most important voice of democratic opinion in the country. But after five stormy months, increasingly harassed by the state censor and the paper's bourgeois shareholders, he was forced to resign, and the publication folded soon afterward.

Another offer to edit a periodical was not long in coming. This time it was Arnold Ruge, a fellow Young Hegelian, who needed Marx's help with a new journal of radical philosophy and social criticism. In order to emphasize what both regarded as the complementary affinity of French political maturity and German philosophical sophistication, the journal was given the high-sounding name of *Deutsch-Französische Jahrbücher*.[1] Since censorship excluded Germany as a place of publication, Paris was chosen for its relatively liberal press laws and its large community of German exiles. In October, 1843, Marx, accompanied by Jenny von Westphalen, his bride, crossed the border to begin the first exile abroad.

The fourteen months he spent in the French capital probably constituted the most crucial period of Marx's formative years. Here he totally immersed himself in the study of contemporary social and economic literature. By his own admission, he still knew little about modern French historiography, socialism, and economic theory. In Paris he read the works of prominent historians like Guizot and Thierry and was impressed by their view that major political events and movements are largely reflections of economic class struggles. At this time, Marx also became acquainted with the theories of three utopian socialists—Saint-Simon, Fourier, and Proudhon—whose vision of a new social order based on fundamental changes in the distribution of socio-economic resources undoubtedly influenced the development of his thought.

Saint-Simon stressed the role of economics in the historical process, insisting that social and political institutions must be evaluated in terms of their ability to deal with the outstanding problems of the day. He argued that in order to eliminate poverty, exploitation, and unemployment, the old order, based on the dominant position of the nobility and the military, has to give way to a new system administered by the men of science, who alone possess the necessary knowledge and moral courage to reorganize natural resources, property, and labor into a new, harmonious relationship intended to benefit the entire society.

Fourier developed his utopian scheme as an antidote to the twin evils of industrial revolution: centralized bureaucracy and capitalism. He proposed to divide the world into many small self-governing and self-supporting units (phalanxes) in which all natural resources and means of production would be commonly owned and production profits would be equitably distributed among labor, capital, and talent. Fourier believed that the realization of his system would free individuals from unnecessary, exploitative labor and enable them to devote considerably more time to the enjoyment of life through creative intellectual pursuits.

Proudhon regarded all forms of collectivism, including the state, property, and the self-governing associations of producers, as being inconsistent with individual freedom. To him various contemporary egalitarian schemes were almost as oppressive as capitalism because they stifled individual initiative, talent, and the capacity to produce. Proudhon's answer to collectivism was a credit system in which individual producers freely and fairly exchange the fruits of their labor. This system presupposes the abolition of all private property except that which is individually or socially useful. In many respects, Proudhon's plan is the most utopian of the three for it is based entirely on universal trust and reciprocity.

IV *The Critic of Hegel*

While still in Germany, Marx began to change his uncritical attitude toward Hegel. The first indication of this change of view is found in his *Critique of Hegel's Philosophy of the State*, completed during Marx's stay at the Westphalen estate in Kreuznach following his marriage to Jenny. Applying the Feuerbachian method, he accuses Hegel of inversion in the subject-predicate relationship and, therefore, rejection of common sense and empirical evidence. "As the Idea [of the state] is subjectivized, the the actual subjects—civil society, family, 'circumstances, caprice, etc.'—become *unactual* objective moments of the Idea," [2] or predicates of an abstraction that has no relation to human reality.

Hegel defines the state as a unity between its universal aims and the particular interests of the individuals, leaving no doubt that, in case of conflict between the two, the former supersedes the latter. Marx sees in this concept the projection of ordinary political life into a religious abstraction. "Up to now the *political constitution* has been the *religious sphere*, the *religion* of the people's life, the heaven of their universality in contrast to the particular *mundane existence* of their actuality." [3] These false attributes of the idealized state reflect a political alienation which, according to Marx, can be overcome only by democracy, in which the true unity of the universal and the particular exists and in which the state itself "is only a self-determination of the people and a particular content of the people." [4] In a democracy man's substance returns to him because the state is his own creation, designed to serve his interests. [5]

In two essays—*On the Jewish Question* and *Toward the Cri-*

tique of Hegel's Philosophy of Law: Introduction—written late in 1843 and published in the only issue of the *Deutsch-Franzö-sische Jahrbücher* (February, 1844), Marx pursues his Feuerbachian criticism of Hegel's social philosophy and expands his own notions on alienation and the prospects of human emancipation.

In *On the Jewish Question*, he argues that the democratization of the state does not, after all, resolve alienation but merely transfers it from the political to the social sphere. Whereas the previous political conflict was between an abstract state and "real" men, in a democracy it is between man as a citizen, "a communal being," and man as a member of civil society, a private individual who "treats other men as means, reduces himself to a means, and becomes a plaything of alien powers." [6]

In the society of an emancipated state, money turns out to be the secular creed, which Marx equates with Judaism:

> Money is the jealous god of Israel before whom no other god may exist. Money degrades all the gods of mankind—and converts them into commodities. Money is the general, self-sufficient *value* of everything. Hence it has robbed the whole world, the human world as well as nature, of its proper worth. Money is the alienated essence of man's labor and life, and this alien essence dominates him as he worships it.
>
> The god of the Jews has been secularized and has become the god of the world. The bill of exchange is the Jew's actual god. His god is only an illusory bill of exchange. [7]

Christianity, an offspring of Judaism, also reflects greed and the worship of money as the principal forces in civil society. But at least in one respect the progeny is even worse than the progenitor:

> Judaism reaches its height with the perfection of civil society, but civil society achieves perfection only in the *Christian* world. Only under the reign of Christianity, which makes *all* national, natural, moral, and theoretical relationships external to man, was civil society able to separate itself completely from political life, sever all man's species-ties, substitute egoism and selfish need for those ties, and dissolve the human world into a world of atomistic, mutually hostile individuals. [8]

Marx predicts that human alienation will be overcome when man is able to transcend the cleavage between his political altruism and private egoism by applying the former to his everyday life as a member of the civil society.[9]

In *Toward the Critique of Hegel's Philosophy of Law: Introduction*, Marx declares that Feuerbach's critique of religion "ends with the doctrine that *man is the highest being for man*, hence with the *categorical imperative to overthrow all conditions* in which man is a degraded, enslaved, neglected, contemptible human being." [10] But in order to achieve this goal one should not depend on criticism alone, for the "weapon of criticism obviously cannot replace the criticism of weapons. Material force must be overthrown by material force." [11] Such force is provided by a class whose unparalleled suffering encompasses all existing social ills and produces an irrevocable determination to eliminate, once and for all, the causes of its own and, therefore, of all mankind's plight. In other words, the interests of this most revolutionary class and those of humanity coincide because by liberating itself it liberates everybody else, even the oppressors. In the *Introduction*, Marx is already convinced that the only class that is qualified for this historical role is the proletariat.[12]

In the two critiques of Hegel's philosophy and *On the Jewish Question*, all written during the second half of 1843, Marx increasingly begins to view socioeconomic factors as the principal cause of alienation. Although, at times, he still seems to regard religion and politics in the same category as economics,[13] the thrust of his thought is that the causes of alienation are to be found in civil society, an arena of human struggle dominated by socioeconomic forces. Thus, religious suffering is gradually reduced to a mere reflection of "real suffering," and politics is said to be "in actual fact" the serf of financial power. On the other hand, Marx views money as the real ruler of the world and as the expression of "the alienated essence of man's labor and life." [14] Finally, in what might be the author's most significant attempt thus far to explain human misery in economic terms, he suggests that one of the reasons why the proletariat alone is qualified to assume the historical mission of emancipation is that it demands "the negation of private property." [15]

During the summer of 1844, Marx wrote his famous *Economic and Philosophic Manuscripts*, in which he explicitly identifies labor and its product as causes of alienation. He begins by asserting that in a private property system the object of man's work becomes external to him because the product of his labor inevitably develops into an independent and alien power. In fact, man becomes the slave of his own creation insofar as he has to work in order to subsist. Similarly, work itself must be regarded as alien to the laborer, for it is not a happy occasion in which an individual expresses his nature by a burst of spontaneous creativity, but a dismal necessity forced upon him by others.[16]

Alienated labor and its product lead to a third dimension of alienation. Man is "a species-being," says Marx, because through free, conscious activity he objectifies himself in nature. But when the object of the worker's labor is separated from him, he is deprived of his "species-life," or his human essence. Moreover, alienation "from his species-existence means that one man is alienated from another just as each man is alienated from human nature." [17] Thus, alienated labor results in alienated humanity.

Alienation is overcome by abolishing its original cause, private property. As long as it exists, human beings are obsessed with the acquisition of things without regard for others and their needs. The abolition of private property allows man to realize his full potential as a social being. Now the object of man's labor is no longer an alien power that enslaves him but a true expression of himself, his identification with nature. This "complete and conscious restoration of man to himself" Marx calls communism.[18] In *Economic and Philosophic Manuscripts*, he takes a giant step toward an exclusively economic explanation of alienation. Yet, at this point his economic approach still lacks an empirical basis or a historical perspective and, therefore, in many respects is as abstract as the speculative philosophy of Hegel, which he was now denouncing with increasing vigor.

V Marx and Engels

Friedrich Engels was born in 1820 in the industrial Rhenish town of Barmen, where his father was a prosperous manufacturer of textiles. His education was limited to secondary school, the army, and an apprenticeship in a textile mill. Eventually, Engels settled down as an employee in his father's factory in Manchester, England, and remained there until his retirement.

As a young man, Engels became a follower of Hegel, joined the Hegelian Left, and under the influence of Feuerbach substituted materialism for idealism as the basis of the Hegelian dialectic. He first met Marx in November, 1842, and their meeting was far from cordial. On his way to England, Engels had stopped at the editorial offices of the *Rheinische Zeitung* for a chat with the man who was rapidly gaining a reputation as the leading spokesman of the democratic forces in the Rhineland. Marx's cool reception of his future intellectual partner was the result of Engels's association with a group of Young Hegelians known as the "Freemen," who bitterly scorned Marx's newspaper for its allegedly moderate positions on various political and social issues.

Despite the coolness of their first encounter, the two soon began to correspond, and Engels agreed to contribute articles to the *Rheinische Zeitung* and the *Deutsch-Französische Jahrbücher*. These developments helped them discover their mutual interests and concerns and eventually led to their second meeting, in Paris (September, 1844). This meeting lasted ten days, and out of it emerged a friendship that lasted until Marx's death. The endurance of their collaboration is all the more remarkable in view of the fact that Marx was not the easiest person to befriend or work with.

The joint efforts of Marx and Engels gave the world an ideology known as Marxism. By Engel's own account, Marx played a decisive role in the conception and formulation of its major principles, but the younger partner's habitual deference to Marx oversimplifies the complex nature of their intellectual relationship. There is little doubt that Marx was blessed with a more original and powerful intellect. But it is equally true that without Engels he most probably would not have produced the works that constitute the essence of Marxism. The fundamentals of historical materialism and the scientific proof of their validity were conceived by Marx, but in this as in many other instances Engels was the indispensable man who supplied ideas and facts that significantly influenced Marx's thought. Furthermore, Engels possessed a more orderly mind, well attuned to the realities of life, and enjoyed a greater facility for lucid written expression; these attributes equipped him for the crucial role of authoritative interpreter and clarifier of Marx's more obscure and disjointed concepts. Finally, Engels did make a number of original contributions to Marxism, such as his theories on the dialectics of nature and the evolution of the state.

From the very beginning of their friendship, Engels began to exert influence on Marx. Before the Paris meeting, Engels had spent nearly two years working in the English textile mill. Here the young radical observed the capitalist system at close range and became acutely aware of its many contradictions and the pervasiveness of economic factors in a modern society. These experiences in Britain resulted in a comprehensive study of the effects of capitalism on the proletariat: *The Condition of the Working Class in England in 1844* (*Die Lage der arbeitenden Klassen in England, 1844*), written between November, 1844, and March, 1845. The book contains much shocking evidence of proletarian suffering and exploitation; denunciations of the ruling classes; and a prediction of bloody class wars unless the communists, by increasing their power among the workers, could carry out a social revolution without violence.

Marx's interest in political economy developed at approximately the same time but became a major preoccupation only in 1844. *Economic and Philosophic Manuscripts* was preceded by voluminous reading of classic economists, especially Smith, Ricardo, Mill, and Say. Moreover, his frequent visits to the Parisian working-class districts brought Marx into direct contact with some of the worst aspects of capitalism. But despite this exposure to economic theory and practice, Marx continued to be "philosophically" oriented: his theses still rested on empirically unproven assumptions, and his terminology was hopelessly saturated with abstractions. Also, Marx's approach to the study of economics was primarily theoretical and as yet without any clear implications regarding his previously enunciated positions on other subjects.

Engels, on the other hand, produced a factual and interpretative analysis of the British economic system in *The Condition of the Working Class in England in 1844* and an incisive commentary on some of its defenders and critics, contained in two articles, "The Situation in England" ("Die Lage Englands") and "Outlines of a Critique of National Economy" ("Umrisse zu einer Kritik der Nationalökonomie"), published in the *Deutsch-Französische Jahrbücher*. Engels's ideas and his clarity of expression injected a healthy dose of realism into Marx's abstract concepts and most likely prompted him to view economics as an empirical framework that integrated his heretofore loose notions on philosophy, history, economics, and society into a coherent body of thought.

[27]

VI *Transition to Historical Materialism*

During the last months of 1844, Marx and Engels produced their first joint work, *The Holy Family, or Critique of Critical Critique*. Although Marx wrote most of the book, important portions of it unmistakably reflect Engels's influence. The authors' announced objective was to discredit the speculative idealism of the Young Hegelians, and they accomplished this with a vengeance. The significance of the work lies not so much in its polemic aspects, however, but in Marx's and Engels's application of the Hegelian dialectic to the socioeconomic content of the historical process. Private property and the proletariat are represented as opposite poles in an antithesis. Both are forced to act by virtue of their respective situations in an alienated world. The property owner supports the antithesis because to him property represents "power," "comfort," and "the semblance of human existence." To the proletarian, on the other hand, the status quo means only the conditions of slavery, which he is determined to change. Since the plight of humanity is reflected in the suffering of the proletariat, its emancipation signifies the end of alienation.[19]

The Holy Family was written during the period of Marx's transition from the Feuerbachian humanism of his formative years to the maturity of historical materialism. At this time, the basic premises are still Feuerbach's, but the emphasis is clearly shifting to economics and the dialectic. This process reaches another phase in the *Theses on Feuerbach*, a brief but important work written by Marx shortly after his expulsion from France in January, 1845.[20]

Marx once referred to Feuerbach as the true conqueror of the old philosophy. He fully endorsed Feuerbach's view that the starting point of philosophy ought to be man, not an abstract category, and regarded his critique of religion as the basis of all criticism. But as he indicated in his earlier essays, Marx was not content with theoretical criticism, especially if limited solely to religion. He visualized philosophy not only as a means toward the acquisition of knowledge but also as a potent weapon in the struggle for human emancipation. Consequently, in his *Theses* Marx accuses Feuerbach of failing to relate theory to practice and goes so far as to suggest that only in "practice man must prove the truth." He also argues that merely to point out the secular basis of religion is not enough; instead, one should try to change the conditions in the secular world that have caused men to engage in religious self-deception. Finally, Marx believes that Feuerbach's refusal to go beyond religious alienation led him to regard man as "species," or an abstraction totally isolated from the real conditions of life.[21]

The young Marx attempted to solve the problem of alienation by identifying and attacking the root causes of human misery. He agreed with Feuerbach that the speculative idealism of Hegel was reflecting, as well as obscuring, the fact of man's loss of his true self. Relying extensively on the Feuerbachian method of subject-predicate transposition, Marx showed that Hegel's philosophy related to the real conditions of life only insofar as it rationalized the misery of the oppressed.

To Marx, alienated man was one who, as a result of conditions beyond his control, was unable to express himself freely and creatively as a member of the human community. Originally, he applied this test to the religious, political, social, and economic spheres without any apparent priorities in terms of emphasis. But by 1844 Marx started to move toward the notion that the economic base of society contained all the fundamental causes of alienation. This discovery was given a dialectical dimension, and man became a creature of socioeconomic forces spanning the course of history. Furthermore, Marx began to grow impatient with his contemporaries, who were unwilling to put their theories to the test of practice, and argued that criticism without subsequent action designed to eliminate conditions responsible for existing wrongs is as futile as the speculative idealism itself. Thus the promise of the *Theses* was to be fulfilled; philosophy became an instrument of change.

CHAPTER 2

The Historical Materialist

I   The German Ideology

*T*HE *GERMAN IDEOLOGY* marks the turning point in the evolution of Marx's thought. It was the product of his second joint effort with Engels, although Marx wrote the crucial chapter on Feuerbach in which the principal theses of the book are presented.[1] In this chapter he puts together his previously held views on the Hegelian dialectic, and on history, political economy, society, and classes into a system of ideas, or at least a foundation for one, that, taken as a whole, imbues its individual parts with a new dimension and new meaning. Before he began to work on *The German Ideology*, Marx spent six weeks in England pursuing his studies of English economic literature, observing the most highly developed capitalist economy in action, and making contacts with British socialists. Once back in Brussels, where he and Engels established residence following their expulsion from France, Marx was ready to settle accounts with his "erstwhile philosophic conscience."[2]

In the chapter on Feuerbach, Marx for the first time systematically enunciates the principles of the material conception of history and reinterprets accordingly such concepts as alienation, division of labor, state, society, and others. He views history as a dialectical process that constantly reflects the basic premise of human reality: the need to produce in order to survive. Men's efforts to improve the methods of production inevitably result in the division of labor, which, in turn, is responsible for various contradictions, such as those between manual and intellectual labor, consumption and production, poverty and wealth, and individual and community interests. These economic phenomena, referred to by Marx as productive forces and relations (the two concepts are explained below), determined ideas, social institutions, and the individual's role in society. The roots of human alienation are also found in the division of labor:

> For as soon as labor is distributed, each man has a particular, exclusive sphere of activity, which is forced upon him and from which he cannot escape. He is a hunter, a fisherman, a shepherd, or a critical critic, and must remain so if he does not want to lose his means of livelihood. . . .
> This crystallization of social activity, this consolidation of what we ourselves produce into an objective power above us, growing out of our control, thwarting our expectations, bringing to naught our calculations, is one of the chief factors in the historical development up till now.[3]

Moreover, the separation of the producers (not to be confused with the owners of the means of production) from the instruments and the fruits of their labor deprives them of any meaningful relations with other men and reduces everyone, except the owners, to lifeless abstractions in continuous conflict with one another.[4]

Alienation will be overcome when the division of labor is abolished and all instruments of production are made "subject to each individual, and property to all." According to Marx, the appropriation of the prevailing productive forces involves "nothing more than the development of the individual capacities corresponding to the material instruments of production." Because of the universal character of their class and the fact that they are "completely shut off from all self-activity," or opportunity to express themselves freely in production (thus representing the most direct antithesis to the thesis of the existing productive forces and their principal beneficiaries, the owners), only the proletarians are qualified for this historic mission.

The appropriation of the productive forces also removes restrictions imposed upon man's social nature by the division of labor. Consequently, communism is again presented by Marx as a liberating and humanizing phenomenon:

Only at this stage [communism] does self-activity coincide with material life, which corresponds to the development of individuals into complete individuals and the casting-off of all natural limitations. The transformation of labor into self-activity corresponds to the transformation of the earlier limited intercourse to the intercourse of individuals as such. With the appropriation of the total productive forces through united individuals, private property comes to an end.[5]

Marx insists that his conclusions about history, man, social change, and the future can be empirically verified because they are based on "real, active men and their actual life process." This position is contrasted with the positions of Hegel and Feuerbach: the former is again criticized for his preoccupation with the thought processes, the latter for his abstract, nonhistorical view of man. Yet the influence of both philosophers is still clearly evident in the pages of *The German Ideology*. The concept of alienation, although presented in terms of the division of labor, occupies a prominent place in the book. Also, the principles, if not the assumptions, of the Hegelian dialectic are widely applied to disentangle the process of change within the newly discovered basis of civil society, that is, the political economy.

II *The Materialist Conception of History*

By the time *The German Ideology* was completed, Marx had already assumed that (1) material conditions determine human life; (2) material conditions and, therefore, human life develop according to the principles of the dialectic; (3) man's nature is essentially social and can express itself fully only through free relations with other men; (4) by examining the material history of man, one can discover the forces which not only are responsible for his present plight but also point to an ultimately brighter future; (5) in humanity's progress toward emancipation, the proletariat is destined to play a key historical role; and (6) future society will be free of material restraints on the individual's activities, making it possible for all men to utilize their potential to the utmost.

This set of assumptions and deductions provided the philosophical framework within which Marx developed his critique of capitalism. He was convinced that empirical data without a theoretical frame of reference are as meaningless as philosophy without any basis in fact. In this sense, Marx's subsequent writings, especially his economic studies, achieved the double effect of expanding, detailing, modifying, and clarifying many general themes of the material conception of history, as well as surrounding it with an aura of scientific precision, objectivity, and verifiability. Consequently, although the fundamentals of historical materialism are already found in *The German Ideology*, the complete product emerges only with the appearance of such works as *The Poverty of Philosophy* (1847), *The Communist Manifesto* (1848), *A Contribution to the Critique of Political Economy* (1859), *Capital* (1867), *Critique of the Gotha Program* (1875), and others.

Marx lays the foundations of his materialist theory with several empirically verifiable observations and assumptions. The first assumption of history is that in order to live and "make history" men need food, drink, clothing, and shelter. The first historical action, therefore, is the production of the means to satisfy these basic needs. But as soon as the essential needs are satisfied, new ones arise, requiring new means of production to satisfy them.[6]

Another historical fact (or circumstance as Marx calls it) is that men reproduce themselves. This causes the expansion of population and, with it, the expansion of needs, means of production, and human relationships, all of which eventually results in the division of labor and private property, a development that opens a new era in history:

> The division of labor inside a nation leads at first to the separation of industrial and commercial from agricultural labor, and hence to the separation of town and country and a clash of interests between them. Its further development leads to the separation of commercial from industrial labor. At the same time through the division of labor there develop further, inside these various branches, various divisions among the individuals co-operating in definite kinds of labor. The relative position of these individual groups is determined by the methods employed in agriculture, industry and commerce (patriarchalism, slavery, estates, classes). . . .
> The various stages of development in the division of labor are just so many different forms of ownership; i.e. the existing stage in the division of labor determines also the relations of individuals to one another with reference to the material, instrument, and product of labor.[7]

The division of labor brings about a proliferation of productive forces, collectively known as the mode of production, which encompass the application of labor, science, technology, and raw materials to production.[8] Thus, the productive forces can be said to reflect man's relations with the material means of production or more broadly, with nature. But there is another type of contact in the productive process: "In production men not only act on nature but also on one another. They produce only by co-operating in a certain way and mutually exchanging their activities." [9] Marx calls this cooperation between producing individuals relations of production, which is but a different name for property and class relations.[10]

III *The Theory of Class Struggle*

The relations of production are essentially relations between the owners of the means of production and those who contribute only their labor to the productive process. The two classes reflect the basic social division in all societies in which private property is the prevalent form of ownership; or, putting it differently, they represent various forms of participation in production that evolve into classes with irreconcilably antagonistic interests. The owners of the means of production form the dominant class and resist any changes that may jeopardize their special position in society. The propertyless individuals become members of the oppressed class and, with equal determination, attempt to dislodge the property owners from their seats of economic and political power.[11]

The capitalists and the proletarians represent the division of society based on the productive forces and relations that have developed during the modern era. The owners of the capitalist means of production amass wealth by exploiting the proletarian wage-labor. Marx's theory of surplus value was intended to prove this claim and to show that, without the proletariat, the capitalists could not achieve and maintain their dominant position in society (see Chapter 3 for a more elaborate discussion of this theory). The proletarian also needs the capitalist, however, because the latter is the only available buyer of his sole commodity, labor. The result is that two contradictions are forced to coexist in a temporary union of convenience.

The contemporary production processes and property relations are responsible for class antagonisms in modern societies only. In the past, more primitive production methods and corresponding social relations produced different class divisions: in antiquity, between slave owners and slaves; in the Middle Ages, between feudal lords and serfs.

Within the structure of the two principal antagonists, there are at least three other categories of classes: (1) subdivisions of the two main groups, (2) marginal classes, and (3) service classes. For example, in the first category one will find financiers, manufacturers, and merchants, all of them capitalists, bourgeois, or members of the middle class—the three terms Marx interchangeably used to denote the propertied class during the capitalist period.[12] In the same category one will also find industrial laborers, agricultural workers (landless peasants who work for others), and the so-called *lumpenproletariat*, or workers who sell themselves to the ruling classes—all proletarians. The second category includes the petty bourgeois (small entrepreneurs such as shopkeepers and artisans), whose interests alternatively coincide with those of the capitalists or the proletarians. The third category consists of the professions, the bureaucracy, the armed forces, and the specialists of various types, groups that perform services for the propertied classes.[13]

In Marx's theory, classes both reflect the particular conditions of production and act as human agents of the historical process. Class struggles generate social tensions that result in large-scale upheavals, culminating in the overthrow of the existing socioeconomic order. Marx argues that at the bottom of every significant political, national, religious, or military conflict there is a clash of class interests. For example, the causes of the seventeenth-century English revolutions are to be found not in the religious or dynastic disputes but in the rising aspirations of the bourgeoisie. Similarly, the real issues in the French Revolution were not the royal abuse of power or the rights of the individuals but the attempt by the bourgeoisie to dislodge the traditional classes, the nobility and the clergy, from their dominant positions in society.

IV The Structure and the Superstructure

The relations of production, which Marx calls "the economic structure, the real foundation" of society, give rise to a legal and political superstructure and "corresponding forms of social consciousness."[14] This means that society's legal system, social and political institutions, moral code, philosophical outlook, and various subjectively creative manifestations such as art and literature are determined by the particular relationships men enter among themselves and, ultimately, by the material means they use in the production process: "The mode of production of material life conditions the social, political, and intellectual life process in general," declared Marx in a famous paragraph from the preface to *A Contribution to the Critique of Political Economy*.[15] In a letter to a friend he elaborated on the relationship between the structure and the superstructure:

> Assume a particular state of development in the productive forces of man and you will get a particular form of commerce and consumption. Assume particular stages of development in production, commerce and consumption and you will have a corresponding social constitution, a corresponding organization of the family, of orders or of classes, in a word, a corresponding civil society. Assume a particular civil society and you will get particular political conditions which are only the official expression of civil society.[16]

In the superstructure, the propertied classes use the state to extend their domination over all spheres of human endeavor, including the intellectual: "The class which has the means of material production at its disposal, has control at the same time over the means of mental production, so that . . . the ideas of those who lack the means of mental production are subject to it." [17]

Marx's interpretation of society in terms of the economic structure and the noneconomic superstructure lacks precision and consistency. He and Engels frequently contradict themselves in defining the relationship and the composition of the two phenomena. At times both the relations and the forces of production are said to constitute the structure; at other times, the forces seem to be excluded from it.[18] Similarly, although the thrust of their pronouncements clearly assigns the structure to a dominant position vis-à-vis the superstructure, occasionally they imply that political institutions and other noneconomic factors may exercise considerable influence on the course of economic development.[19] Lastly, Marx's and Engels's relatively few attempts to explain the more distant history on the basis of structure-superstructure relationships are hazy, haphazard, and incomplete. Nowhere in their writings can one find a clear or consistent identification of the forces and relations of production, and the corresponding superstructures, during antiquity and the Middle Ages. But despite these ambiguities in his conceptual framework, there is no doubt that Marx views the production process as a key element in the social evolution of man and manmade institutions. The notion of close but unequal relationship between economic phenomena and human progress (sometimes referred to as "economic determinism") plays a crucial role in his explanation of historical change and man's destiny.

V *The Process of History*

In Marx's view, the history of civilization rests on the dialectical relationship between the mode and the relations of production, the former constituting a determining factor in this union of opposites. At certain periods in history, due to innovations in the production techniques, the discovery of new raw materials, an expansion of world commerce, or a combination of all three, man's relations with the material means of production (mode of production) undergo a change, triggering corresponding changes in his relations with other men engaged in production (relations of production). A new machine, such as a loom powered by steam, requires not only a different application and organization of labor but also a new relationship between the manager and the worker, as well as the property owner and the propertyless individual. The power loom and similar newly introduced machines are responsible for the emergence of modern mass production with all the attendant changes: assemblage of large numbers of workers into new production units, factories, run by professional managers and owned by stockholders. The new mode sharply contrasts with the old (feudal) when the material means of production consisted of primitive machines powered by water, wind, or human hands, and when production was scattered among many small units, estates or workshops, owned and operated by lords or guild masters and, in most cases, employing no more than several dozen serfs or workers. Thus, Marx could proclaim that the "handmill gives you society with the feudal lord; the steam-mill, society with the industrial capitalist." [20]

The establishment of a new society (new class and property relations, or relations of production), based on a new mode of production, requires a new set of legal, political, and social institutions, as well as philosophical doctrines, moral codes, and aesthetic forms, to promote, protect, and rationalize the new socio-economic order and the interests of its dominant class.

The transition from one socioeconomic order to another is usually not a smooth one. Conflict is caused by the fact that the mode of production and the relations of production do not change simultaneously. Changes in the latter always lag behind those in the former. Thus, the new means of production must temporarily put up with the old class and property relations and their supporting noneconomic institutions, ideological systems, and aesthetic forms. Although the old relations are eventually replaced by new ones which are compatible with the operating mode of production, they continue to resist change until the very end and thereby cause large-scale upheavals, or social revolutions. Marx regarded the seventeenth-century British and the eighteenth-century French revolutions as social revolutions in which the bourgeoisie started the process of developing its own relations of production and the corresponding institutional and ideological superstructures. The historical necessity for a compatible modes and relations of production is described by Engels as follows:

The mode of production peculiar to the bourgeoisie, known, since Marx, as the capitalist mode of production, was incompatible with the local privileges and the privileges of estate as well as with the reciprocal personal ties of the feudal system. The bourgeoisie broke up the feudal system and built upon its ruins the capitalist order of society, the kingdom of free competition, of personal liberty, of the equality, before the law, of all commodity owners, of all the rest of the capitalist blessings. Thenceforward the capitalist mode of production could develop in freedom.[21]

Through free political institutions and legal safeguards of individual rights, modern democracy guarantees free development of the capitalist mode of production and establishes wealth as a dominant force in politics, two characteristics which make it more compatible with the interests of the ruling bourgeoisie than any previous political system.[22] Not surprisingly, therefore, democracy appears soon after the victory of the capitalist system of production and remains the prevalent form of state during the bourgeois period. Other components of the old (feudal) superstructure also undergo changes designed to increase the power of the class that owns the new means of production. The medieval family, formed by prearranged marriages in which tradition played a key role, gives way to a bourgeois family based on the consent and equality of both partners. In reality, however, the new family is neither free nor equal as far as the role of women is concerned, but it suits the bourgeois class interests by permitting marriages arising from purely economic considerations, and by helping to promote a wider and more direct exploitation of female and child labor.[23] In religion, the gradual ascendance of the capitalist mode of production results in the loss of secular power by the Catholic Church, the mainstay of the feudal system, and the introduction of more liberal versions of Christianity. The disintegration of centralized religious authority liberates philosophy, jurisprudence, art, literature, and science from theology and permits their full utilization by the rising bourgeoisie. Furthermore, liberalized Christianity, especially in its Protestant form, directly promotes the interests of the new ruling class by supplying religious rationalizations for individual initiative and responsibility, inviolability of private property, and rejection of social altruism.[24]

The transition from one socioeconomic order to another may last for a considerable time because "new, higher relations of production never appear before the material conditions of their existence have matured in the womb of the old society itself." [25] Thus, although the first stirrings of the capitalist mode of production in the West surfaced as early as the sixteenth century, following the discovery of new continents and a rapid expansion of international commerce, the capitalist relations of production developed fully only in the nineteenth century after the introduction of new production techniques.[26]

Marx identifies four past and present modes of production and their socioeconomic orders: Asiatic or primitive communist, ancient or classical, feudal or medieval, and bourgeois or capitalist.[27] The first mode is characterized by the use of the most primitive instruments of production (made out of stone and later iron), communal property, division of labor based on age and sex, and the production of goods for communal consumption.[28] The last three modes are predicated on private property ownership and control of production, exploitation of the many by the few, and bitter class antagonism. Moreover, they contain self-destroying contradictions. Marx was convinced that, under capitalism, social ills emanating from private property would reach unprecedented extremes. Although capitalist production is socialized (large numbers of people participate in the production process), its fruits are appropriated by few individuals (the owners of the means of production).[29] Consequently, everything in a capitalist society is subordinated to the accumulation of wealth: the public interest is sacrificed to class interest; the working and living conditions of labor, to individual profit; the economic stability and progress of the country, to the exigencies of competition. Such unrestricted pursuit of profit, constantly reinforced by the knowledge that failure to survive capitalist competition means the exit from the ranks of the dominant class, necessitates periodic contractions in production followed by progressively increasing misery of the proletariat.[30] These circumstances make the steady expansion and improvement of the productive forces virtually impossible and, therefore, the removal of the capitalist conditions of production imperative. The change comes about when the working class, desperate in its utter misery, seizes political power and establishes what Marx called the dictatorship of the proletariat. This political system is, at the same time, a state and a period of transition between communism and capitalism.[31] Like all states, it serves the interests of the ruling class and oppresses its opponents. The only difference is that, in this case, the ruling class, i.e., the proletariat, represents a majority of the population, and the oppressed class, the bourgeoisie, only a small minority. The new regime eliminates the basic capitalist contradiction by transferring the means of production from private to public ownership. From then on, the fruits of the collective effort in the production process will be shared by all participants in an equitable way determined by the nature of work and individual need. The disappearance of private property will also restore a harmonious relationship between the forces and relations of production, once again releasing the former to unhindered and rapid development.

VI *The Millennium*

Marx assumes that harmony in the productive process will be reflected in the society at large, in which the abolition of individual ownership will render the existence of social classes and their supporting institutions, ideologies, and creative intellectual manifestations superfluous. The elimination of the principal causes of human misery and conflict will also release formerly unrealized human capacities to the utmost, thus freeing man from the slavery of his material environment. In social life, coercion, best exemplified by the state and its many subdivisions, will be replaced by cooperation and voluntary association, concepts which Marx most probably borrowed from the French utopian socialists. Neither he nor Engels, however, was very specific on what was to follow the dictatorship of the proletariat. As in the case of this dictatorship itself, they left only a few general outlines and virtually no details as far as the future stages of history were concerned.[32] It is quite possible that the founders of Marxism failed to elaborate on their predictions simply because, public utterances notwithstanding, they were not all that sure as to the exact nature and sequence of future developments and did not want to be contradicted by history in their own lifetimes. It is also possible that Marx and Engels were only interested in the historical logic of their predictions and, therefore, decided to ignore the potentially embarrassing details. Both explanations have a certain amount of plausibility but, needless to say, they have been of little help either to the practitioners of Marx's and Engels's doctrines or to scholars who have sought clarity and consistency in Marxist thought.

The propertyless, classless, and stateless society of the future, in which social harmony and individual freedom are dominant characteristics, Marx calls communism. Once it is realized, the Marxist social dialectic, based on conflict and contradiction, will lose its autodynamic force and cease to be a vehicle of historical change and progress. The arrival of communism will signify that the "mission" of the dialectic has been accomplished because, as M. M. Bober has pointed out, Marx, in a truly Hegelian fashion, viewed history as a progressive march to freedom that finds its ultimate realization in the socialized mode of production, a Marxist variant of Hegel's Absolute Idea.[33]

Thus, to the early "humanist," as well as to the later "materialist" Marx, emancipation meant man's liberation from the slavery of the alien material forces grounded in the system of private property. The major difference between the two Marxes lies neither in the vision of the future nor in the causes of alienation, but rather in the reinterpretation of this concept in terms of contemporary social conditions and a comprehensive explanation of

[41]

the circumstances of its eventual disappearance as a human problem. The early Marx, although already emphasizing the role of private property in the dehumanization of man, was still applying an essentially nonhistorical, and largely philosophical, approach to alienation. The Marx of the materialist period, on the other hand, modified his approach by deemphasizing the philosophical content in favor of the socioeconomic one and by adding a historical dimension in the form of Herculean efforts to identify and define the various historical forces and conditions leading toward the millennium. In this sense, it is possible to argue convincingly on both sides of the issue whether, in terms of theoretical thought, there were two or only one Marx—a phenomenon amply illustrated in recent literature on the subject.

CHAPTER 3

The Economist:
Materialist Philosophy Elaborated

I Philosophical Foundations

IN the preceding chapter, I pointed out that Marx's economic studies constitute an integral part of his materialist philosophy and, therefore, can be meaningfully evaluated only within the context of its major presuppositions. Although he detested economics as a dull and frustrating science and occasionally used colorful epithets to describe it, Marx was convinced that economic factors, stemming from basic human needs, were paramount in man's individual and social evolution. But before he permanently settled in London in 1849, his numerous involvements in illegal political activities and revolutionary propaganda left him with little time for the study of economics. Before 1849 his exposure to the subject was largely limited to secondary sources—the writings of contemporary economists such as Ricardo, Sismondi, Say, and others. Thus, when Marx's exile in England temporarily removed him from the whirlpool of European revolutionary politics, he could finally turn his undivided attention to that dull and frustrating science. There is considerable evidence, however, suggesting that, for the author of *Capital*, the preoccupation with economic studies during the early years of his English exile constituted one of the most trying periods of his life. First of all, Marx's innovative mind and tempestuous personality were ill suited for the rigors of a seemingly endless sifting of factory inspectors' reports and similar economic data. Second, the immersion in economic studies subjected his growing family to prolonged and consistent hardships. Finally, these two factors contributed to the gradual deterioration of his own health and effectiveness as the ideological and, sometimes, organizational leader of the incipient international proletarian movement.

In *The German Ideology*, Marx and Engels declared their theoretical premises to be rooted in "real individuals, their activity and the material conditions under which they live" and, therefore, verifiable "in a purely empirical way." [1] Essentially the same notion was reaffirmed by Marx some fourteen years later when, in the preface to *A Contribution to the Critique of Political Economy* (1859), he pointed out that "the material transformation of the economic conditions of production . . . can be determined with the precision of natural science." [2] Hence, Marx's economic studies might be considered as an effort to test the validity of his materialist philosophy against pertinent empirical data. He did not, however, approach the subject matter with the detachment of a scientist interested only in finding the truth regardless of what it may do to his hypotheses. On the contrary, Marx firmly believed that the truth had already been discovered and was embodied in the theory of historical materialism and the methodology of the dialectic. The work on *Capital*, its author declared, was undertaken with the objective "to lay bare the economic law of motion of modern society." [3]

In his economc works, Marx applied his materialist philosophy to economic phenomena in order to strengthen its scientific credibility and social impact. For example, he selected and evaluated data in terms of dialectical contradictions constantly resolving themselves into new entities, marshaled impressive evidence behind such propositions as the inherently exploitative nature of wage labor, and constructed new theories demonstrating the inevitable disintegration of capitalism. In short, methodologically and substantively, Marx's economic studies were but an extension of historical and dialectical materialism and not a repository of empirical verification. On the other hand, it is not surprising that the enormous accumulation of data and their manipulation in order to construct new theorems and concepts in *Capital* and other major works easily created the impression of scientific objectivity, precision, and finality, and tended to endow the philosophical theory—in his post-*Capital* writings often referred to by Engels as "scientific socialism"—with all the prestige and impact enjoyed by science in the modern world.

Thus, it appears that Marx's interest in economics stemmed directly from his philosophical premises developed during the mid-1840s. But why did he concentrate almost exclusively on the subject of capitalism, largely ignoring other contemporary or past economic systems? After all, Marx agreed that the historical process was not a series of accidental occurrences but a train of consecutive events, dialectically set in motion and developing according to the material laws of history. This process was supposed to encompass the entire human reality, that is, all individuals in terms of time and place who come into contact with other individuals in the process of fulfilling their basic human needs. Hence capitalism, or any other economic system, is just a fragment or a phase in the totality of the historical process. How, then, does one explain Marx's disproportionate emphasis on capitalism as a model of explication of his materialist philosophy?

There was one practical reason that may have had something to do with Marx's decision to pursue a comprehensive study of capitalism. Because of his revolutionary activities in 1848, he was no longer welcome in most European countries and was forced to establish permanent residence across the Channel. In London, the center of the most capitalist country in the world, Marx found large quantities of contemporary economic data that were easily accessible and relevant to the general thrust of his philosophical thought. If he had chosen to do a thorough study of the prevalent economic systems of classical antiquity or the Middle Ages, Marx undoubtedly would have encountered virtually insurmountable obstacles in his efforts to obtain the necessary data because the deeper one reached into the past the scarcer the documentary evidence was likely to become.

But there were other, more basic, reasons for Marx's resolve "to lay bare the economic law of motion of modern society." Essentially, he was interested in the study of the past only insofar as it helped one to understand the present and to predict the future. Marx was genuinely appalled by the social problems of the Industrial Revolution and was determined not to remain passive amidst the moral outrages of his times. Moreover, in capitalism he saw class antagonisms revealed in the most simplified form; [4] this made it easier for him to separate the substantive from the superficial, to disentangle the contradictions of societies based on exploitation, and to identify the historical forces that held promise for a better future.

II *Commodity, Labor, Value, Profit*

Marx's critique of capitalism begins with the definition of commodity as an object outside of us that possesses some usefulness and is a product of labor. Commodities contain two kinds of value, use-value and exchange value, but only through the latter can the value of a commodity be expressed in concrete terms. Furthermore, the source of all value is labor and, therefore, the value of a commodity is measurable by the quantity of labor that has gone into making it. The quantity of labor is, in turn, determined by the amount of time expended on the production of a commodity. But this, if taken literally, would mean that a slow and inexperienced laborer would create more value than a skilled and hard-working one.

Marx explains this difficulty by pointing out that value-creating labor is homogeneous human labor and, as such, cannot be considered individually. It must be viewed as part of the total expenditure of labor power generated by all individual producers and representing the total value embodied in all the commodities produced in a society. Consequently, if one wants to measure the quantity of labor required to produce a given article, one must apply not the measurement of actual expended time but the socially necessary labor time, or what is required to produce the said article with an average skill and intensity and under prevailing conditions of production. As an example, Marx cited the case of the English textile industry. With the introduction of power looms, the labor time required to convert yarn into cloth was cut in half. This meant that the still-operating hand looms continued to absorb an hour of actual labor for what now amounted to a half hour of socially necessary labor and that, therefore, the value of the product fell to one-half of its former value.[5]

The next major question to which Marx addressed himself was the source of the capitalist's profits. If the value of commodities is determined by the socially necessary labor time, their exchange is merely the exchange of equal commodity values. Under such conditions, even if one man cheats and receives more money [6] for his commodities than is warranted by the value of labor put into them, this would either involve a temporary gain (the truth will eventually catch up with a dishonest man) or make little impact on the economy as a whole.

[46]

But if exchange does not result in profits, then where do profits come from? Marx's answer is that one commodity is consistently and significantly underpaid, thereby producing a net gain for its buyer and user. This commodity is labor, which the owner of the means of production buys at the value determined by the average labor time needed to produce it, or, in this instance, for the minimum wages necessary for a worker to sustain himself and to raise and sustain a family. Thus, if it always took a whole day to earn subsistence wages, the question of profits would not arise. But, according to Marx, this is certainly not the case under capitalism. Ordinarily, it takes the producers (his term for the workers engaged in the production of commodities) considerably less than a full day's labor to earn what is necessary for subsistence and procreation; yet everywhere, in Marx's time, they continued to work long hours, at least six days a week.[7] The difference between socially necessary labor, or labor required to secure subsistence, and the actual labor performed by the worker constitutes that portion of labor which is unpaid and produces surplus value. In other words, the capitalist gets something for nothing by forcing the worker to toil longer than he is paid for and pocketing the difference in the form of profits. The concept of surplus value is the key to Marx's contention that capitalism is based on the exploitation of the worker.

In the production of commodities, the capitalist buys labor power (or the quantity of labor as determined by the socially necessary labor time) and sets it to work on different means of production, such as machinery, raw materials, and so forth. Marx calls the first component of the production process variable capital and the second, constant capital. Since labor is the sole value-producing commodity, only variable capital constitutes a source of surplus value. Constant capital, on the other hand, represents various material objects on which labor had been previously expended in order to convert them into the means of production (labor applied to iron ore converts it into an industrial machine). As such, it has certain use-value but, unlike labor, no direct value-creating capacity. Consequently, each capital consists of constant and variable parts, forming what Marx refers to as the organic composition of capital. If constant capital predominates, the composition is "higher"; if the opposite is true, it is "lower." [8] The various ramifications of the relationship between constant and variable capital form one of the principal devices used by Marx to prove the inevitability of the demise of capitalism.

As there are two types of capital, there are also two types of surplus value. One of them depends on the length of the working day, the other on the productivity of the work itself. Absolute surplus value results when the working day is prolonged beyond the point of socially necessary labor, or beyond the value of the worker's labor power. Relative surplus value emanates from increased efficiency in the means of production, or the reduction of the time needed to produce value equivalent to subsistence wages.[9] Thus, surplus value can be achieved through the increase of surplus labor, the decrease of socially necessary labor, or a combination of the two.

III *The Process of Accumulation*

Surplus value is of the utmost importance to the growth of capital. A portion of it is consumed by the capitalist but the rest is accumulated, or reinvested, in order to expand the existing outlays in constant and variable capital. The reasons for the ceaseless accumulation are twofold: one is found in a typical capitalist's desire to amass wealth and power, the other in the necessities of capitalist competition. The first reason is subjective, stemming from such personality traits as "avarice" or the "love of power"; [10] the second is objective, the result of the prevailing material conditions. In order to survive as a member of the privileged power elite, the capitalist must successfully compete with his peers, a task that demands continuous accumulation.[11] In this sense, he is a victim of his own inner drives and of the system in which he operates.[12]

As might be expected, Marx places considerably more emphasis on the objective causes of accumulation. The capitalist means of production do not remain static, but constantly undergo various changes.[13] This is particularly evident in the application of new scientific and technological inventions to the construction of cheaper and more efficient machines. Furthermore, as the capital invested in production expands, so does the division of labor. The twin progress toward greater efficiency in the capitalist mode of production is simultaneous with the rise of labor productivity, a phenomenon that has a direct bearing on modern economic competition.[14]

The struggle for profits forces the capitalists to engage in practices aimed at undermining their competitors. The most effective way to put a wrench into the wheels of other capitalists is to undersell them.[15] However, this can be effectively accomplished only by lowering the production costs which, in turn, depend on the industrialist's ability to increase the productivity of labor. Now, as we have already seen, labor productivity is directly related to mechanization and specialization (or expansion of the division of labor); hence, in order to compete successfully with his rivals, the manufacturer must invest more in machinery and proportionally less in labor power.

Yet, the reduction of the production costs is, at best, only a temporary reprieve for the typical capitalist. Since others are in a similar predicament, they either have already adopted the same methods or will shortly follow suit.[16] All of this means that, as the competition progresses, every owner of the means of production is faced with the continuous necessity to reduce further the production costs through increased investments in constant capital.[17] Thus, the growth of constant capital becomes an important element in the development of capitalism and, in the long run, one of the principal reasons for its disintegration.

Another by-product of accumulation is the concentration and centralization of capital. It will be recalled that accumulation means continuous reinvestment in, and expansion of, constant and variable capital outlays. The rise of labor productivity accelerates the production of surplus value, the sole source of reinvestment funds, and thereby speeds up the expansion of capital. Consequently, "every accumulation becomes the means of new accumulation," and the individual capitals ("concentrations of means of production, with a corresponding command over a larger or smaller labor-army") rapidly increase in size. As a result, large-scale production gradually becomes the trademark of capitalism. Marx calls it the concentration of capital.[18]

Centralization denotes the merger of individual capitals into monopolies or trusts. It occurs when an increasing number of manufacturers fail to survive the competition and are absorbed by others. Marx lists several explanations for this phenomenon, the most important being the ability (mainly because of higher efficiency and greater financial resources) of the large capitals to undersell their smaller rivals. He also concedes that some capitals will voluntarily join others for the purpose of guaranteeing or extending their survival. But whatever the reasons, Marx is firm in his conviction that centralization is an inexorable historical force that gains more impetus with each successive phase in capitalist development; and he suggests that the ultimate result of this process might be the control of entire branches of industry by single capitals.[19]

Still another by-product of accumulation is the creation of surplus population, or an industrial reserve army. As the total capital in a society expands (accelerated by such processes as rising labor productivity, the relative increase of constant capital, and the concentration and centralization of capital) and, with it, the potential labor population, so does the variable capital, but in a steadily declining proportion and without a corresponding rise of the labor force. The latter phenomenon is due to the fact that higher productivity enables the same number of individuals to generate more power than in the past.[20] Thus, a wide gap gradually develops between the demand for, and the availability of, new jobs. This process eventually leads to the emergence of a permanent population segment that no longer directly contributes to the expansion of capital and therefore becomes "surplus" or "reserve." Yet, indirectly, it performs an important function in the development of the capitalist mode of production. Marx pointed out that the surplus population provides the manufacturers with a pool of reserve laborers who are available at a moment's notice to meet the needs of unanticipated and sudden expansion of production.[21] The industrial reserve army also serves as an effective reminder to workers that they could easily be replaced by the many unemployed waiting for just such an opportunity outside the gates of the factory. In the short run, this kind of leverage empowers the capitalists to intensify exploitation without fear of adverse consequences.[22]

IV   The Declining Rate of Profit and the Future of Capitalism

But perhaps the most ominous by-product of capitalist accumulation is the tendency of the profit rate to fall. We have already discussed the reasons for the relative decline of variable capital within total capital investments. Since it represents the sole source of profits, or "living labor, unpaid and congealed in surplus value," the decrease of variable capital in relation to constant capital results in a corresponding decrease in the rate of profit, although this does not necessarily mean a decline of the total surplus value, the total variable capital, or the total profit.[23] Nevertheless, Marx was convinced that, eventually, the tendency of the profit rate to fall would lead to the disintegration of capitalism.

He explained, and to his own satisfaction proved, the validity of this thesis through a combination of philosophical argument and selective empirical data. As Marx saw it, one of the principal contradictions of capitalism is the conflict between its historical mission and its practice, or between the unrestricted development of the capitalist forces of production and the imperatives of accumulation. Capitalism starts out as a progressive historical force that revolutionizes existing methods of production by introducing modern techniques designed to make full use of available human and material resources.[24] But the owners of the means of production are not motivated by social altruism; instead, they gradually become prisoners of their material surroundings, and their human, or social, instincts are overwhelmed by the compulsion to amass wealth. A typical capitalist is primarily concerned about the expansion of capital and his survival in the face of competition with other capitalists, rather than the utmost utilization of the productive forces and the equitable distribution of their greatly increased output among all segments of the population. In order to expand his capital and to survive competition, he must raise the productivity of labor—a development which, in turn, induces a higher composition of capital and an inevitable decline in the rate of profit.

Marx wondered why, in view of the tremendous mechanization of the means of production during the capitalist period, the decrease in the profit rate had not been even faster and suggested that this was probably due to a number of counteracting forces. First of all, the capitalists accelerate the exploitation of workers by lengthening the working day and intensifying labor. This enables them to appropriate more surplus value and to recover a portion of the diminishing profit. Second, in many instances the manufacturers arbitrarily lower wages, which achieves essentially the same effect. Third, the rapid expansion of constant capital does not result in a corresponding rise in its value (cost) because of the general reduction in commodity prices, including those of the means of production. In other words, the rise in the organic composition of capital produces built-in savings in production costs. Finally, the emergence of the industrial reserve army, a virtually inexhaustible supply of readily available cheap labor, makes it possible for many capitalists to retain the old, high surplus-value yield production methods alongside the new ones.[25]

Yet, despite the countervailing factors, the profit rate continues to plunge and eventually reaches a phase which Marx calls an "overproduction of capital." The immediate causes of the "overproduction of capital" are the increased productivity of labor and the temporary rises in workers' wages.[26] During this phase, the capital is no longer able to yield enough profit for further expansion, thus forcing the owners of the means of production to adopt what ultimately will prove to be self-destructive measures.[27] The most important of them is the depreciation of capital, or the withdrawal of portions of it from the production process in order to eliminate overproduction of commodities and to reduce the costs of production by laying off some workers and compelling others to accept lower wages. Whose capital and how much of it is to be taken out of production is determined by a fierce competition among the capitalists, generally with the smaller ones losing out.[28] It is not surprising, therefore, that restricted production results in a severe economic crisis marked by industrial stagnation, bankruptcies, and increased unemployment. However, the crisis does not last forever; the deliberate depression of productive forces returns the economy to conditions under which profit-making and accumulation can be resumed, and production begins to expand again. But now the capitalist system finds itself in a cycle from which, in the long run, there is no escape. The resumption of accumulation again leads to the overproduction of capital, which, in turn, necessitates the imposition of restrictions on production.[29]

These periodic crises further expose and deepen the contradictions of capitalism: (1) The hardships of the proletariat increase in scope and intensity. The industrial reserve army continues to swell because the artificially contracted economy fails to keep pace with the constantly growing population. Thus, as the number of potential workers steadily rises, the available jobs fluctuate between sharp decline and slight increase.[30] (2) The problems of unemployment and exploitation become even greater when the capitalists who fail to survive the competition are thrown into the ranks of the proletariat. This puts more unemployed into the already depressed job market and invests the surviving capitalists with additional leverage over the workers. (3) Perhaps the most serious result of the crises caused by the declining rate of profit is their effect on the spirit of capitalism. Profit is capitalism's principal moving force, and when it is no longer attainable the incentive to produce disappears. The enormous concentration and centralization of capital in the hands of the few enable them to manipulate the economy in such a way as to preserve a portion of the declining profit and to prolong their own and the system's survival.[31] This is only a temporary reprieve, however, because during the final phase of capitalism no new capitals emerge and the old ones cannot significantly expand to meet the growing demand for new jobs and improved working and living conditions. Consequently, it appears to be only a matter of time when the gap between the requirements of society and the performance of capitalism will become so wide as to precipitate the latter's breakdown and replacement by a superior socioeconomic system.

The contradiction between capitalism's historical mission to develop fully the material forces of production and the means (the expansion of capital) adopted to that end is what prompted Marx to say that capitalism establishes its own barriers.[32] Although he did not specifically state so, Marx clearly implied that a system which can no longer expand production, and thus meet the minimum demands of society, and, at the same time, protect the interests of the ruling class is doomed to extinction.

V *The End of Capitalism*

Marx was more ambiguous when it came to the identification of the immediate causes and the description of the exact nature of the breakdown of capitalism. Yet, even here the "circumstantial" evidence is fairly revealing. The thrust of his many scattered statements unmistakably supports the notion that the breakdown will come about as a result of prolonged and gradually intensifying economic crises inherent in the system and their cumulative effect on the proletariat.[33] What the capitalist mode of production means to an average proletarian is vividly described by Marx in the first volume of *Capital*:

. . . Within the capitalist system all methods for raising the social pro-
ductiveness of labor are brought about at the cost of the individual
laborer; all means for the development of production transform themselves into means of domination over, and exploitation of, the producers; they mutilate the laborer into a fragment of a man, degrade
him to the level of an appendage of a machine, destroy every remnant
of charm in his work and turn it into a hated toil; they estrange from
him the intellectual potentialities of the labor-process in the same proportion as science is incorporated in it as an independent power; they
distort the conditions under which he works, subject him during the
labor-process to a despotism the more hateful for its meanness; they
transform his life-time into working-time, and drag his wife and child
beneath the wheels of the Juggernaut of capital.[34]

As the capitalist mode of production develops, the lot of the
worker progressively worsens, simultaneously undermining the
very foundations of capitalism: "Along with the constantly diminishing number of the magnates of capital . . . grows the mass of
misery, oppression, slavery, degradation, exploitation; but with
this too grows the revolt of the working-class, a class always increasing in numbers, and disciplined, united, organized by the
very mechanism of the process of capitalist production itself." [35]
Eventually, this process produces socioeconomic conditions in
which the "proletarians have nothing to lose but their chains." At
this time in history, a revolution, born in desperation and unspeakable misery, begins and, before long, results in the overthrow of the capitalist system. Thus, the death of capitalism is
brought about by a combination of material and human causes.
In this situation, the material element acts as a catalyst which
induces the human element to revolutionary action.

VI The Meaning of the Economic Studies

As I have said before, Marx's economic studies were an extension of his materialist philosophy, detailing, elaborating, illus-
trating, and generally giving it a semblance of scientific validity
through the selective use of economic data. A good case in point
is the principal thesis of *Capital*, namely the theory of the declining rate of profit and its effects on the capitalist system. In an
often-quoted summary of the key principles of historical materialism, Marx points out that at "a certain stage of their development, the material productive forces of society come into conflict

with the existing relations of production . . . From forms of development of the productive forces these relations turn into fetters. Then begins an epoch of social revolution." [36] Anyone who has not read *Capital* and understood the full implications of the diminishing profit theory would simply have no idea as to how the relations of production could turn into the fetters of the productive forces. Essentially the same relationship exists between the economic studies and the dialectical part of Marx's philosophy, which is used in *Capital* both as a method to unravel the complexities of socioeconomic phenomena and as an instrument to confirm its own validity as well as to elaborate on its major assumptions.

Thus, Marx explained contemporary economic systems in terms of constant fluctuation between growth and stagnation, abrupt change, contradiction, inner conflict, and progressive disintegration leading toward an inevitable breakdown. Occasionally, he even equated the dialectical categories with economic concepts, apparently to make sure that no one would miss the point as to his methodological approach.[37] Yet, after all is said about the philosophical significance of Marx's greatest work, the fact remains that its impact on humanity has been primarily moral and visionary rather than philosophical or economic. Although Marx did not intend to indict capitalism on moral grounds, the most powerful message of *Capital* concerns the suffering and dehumanization of the masses in a modern, industrial society and the hope for a better future through the disintegration of the system which its author sought to prove as inherently exploitative and self-destructive.

CHAPTER 4

The Revolutionary

I Humanism in Action

AS a young man, Marx displayed many signs that foreshadowed a career of revolutionary activism. The poetry of his youth reflects draconian inner conflicts and a seemingly compulsive urge to assert his own human nature in terms of furious action, whether aimed at breaking out of his self-imposed isolation during the early Berlin days or at advancing the cause of man through attacks on the established order.[1] Just before graduation from the Gymnasium, Marx wrote that "if a person works only for himself he can perhaps be a famous scholar, a great wise man, a distinguished poet, but never a complete, genuinely great man." To achieve greatness, he said, one has to dedicate himself to humanity because "man's nature makes it possible for him to reach his fulfillment only by working for the perfection and welfare of his society."[2] The idea of activist or social humanism resurfaces in other writings of the young Marx. In the foreword to his doctoral dissertation, he praises Prometheus, the rebel who defied the gods in the service of mankind, as the "noblest of saints and martyrs in the calendar of philosophy," and calls man the "supreme divinity."[3]

Immediately after his marriage to Jenny von Westphalen in June of 1843, Marx and his bride moved to the Westphalen estate at Kreuznach, where they remained until their departure for Paris in October of the same year. At the estate, the bridegroom devoted much of his time to writing and reflection. During the *Rheinische Zeitung* and Kreuznach periods, Marx's social humanism acquired a new dimension through journalism and his growing interest in contemporary political and economic issues. His motto was now "ruthless criticism of everything existing,"[4] and he used his position as editor of a liberal newspaper and a radical journal to denounce the Prussian government's authoritarianism and disinterest in the problems of the poor. At this time, however, Marx's criticism was still primarily intended to clarify the confusion arising from conflicting claims of the competing systems and ideologies. He knew that the established order promoted and condoned economic exploitation and the suppression of political freedom, but as yet he was uncertain as to what should be done to eliminate these evils. Marx's ambiguous stand on communism is a good case in point. When accused by the *Augsburger Allgemeine Zeitung* of "flirting with communism," he uncharacteristically refused to pass judgment on the ideology, explaining that it should first be subjected to calm and "thorough criticism." Communism, implied one of the greatest polemicists of his time, is too significant an issue to be evaluated within the context of newspaper polemics.[5]

II *The Early Theory of Revolution*

In Paris, Marx made many acquaintances with European exiles of various ideological persuasions who were waging furious polemical battles against their governments. Here he also continued the intensive study of French socialism and history begun at Kreuznach and, for the first time in his life, came into direct contact with the proletarian class (he frequently attended Parisian workers' meetings and occasionally visited their homes). These experiences were, no doubt, instrumental in crystallizing his views on democracy, communism, the proletariat, and the early theory and strategy of revolution. In *On the Jewish Question, Toward the Critique of Hegel's Philosophy of Law: Introduction,* and in "Critical Notes on 'The King of Prussia and Social Reform,' "[6] he discussed the differences between the state and civil society, between political and social revolutions, and between France and Germany.

Marx declares that the state embodies the contradiction between the general interests of humanity and the particular interests of individual men. The universal character of the state reflects the social nature of man, but its dependence on civil society, in which the private interests of individuals predominate, represents a denial of that same nature. In this sense, the state is faced with a problem similar to that of the alienated man: neither is able to assert its (or his) true nature because of enslavement by alien forces. Consequently, attempts to abolish alienation must be concentrated not on the various political entities but on the socio-economic causes found in civil society. The alienated man will regain his humanity only by abandoning personal egotism in favor of social altruism and thereby resolving the contradiction between public (state) and private (civil society) lives into a synthesis in which principles of public life will be applied to private endeavors.

The assumptions and implications of Marx's concept of alienation lead directly to his theory of revolution. If the root causes of human misery are found in society, then a social revolution will be needed to remove them. Political revolutions, although indispensable in the struggle for radical social change, historically have had little impact on society, generally reflecting—not causing —the realignment of social forces, and usually succeeding only in replacing one state or government with another.[7] In order to change the basic human condition, one has to change its foundation or, what to Marx was one and the same thing, the prevailing socioeconomic system.

If social revolution is the only avenue to human emancipation, then what are its principal instruments? Marx mentions two of them: the proletarian class and philosophy. Individually, neither can perform its historical role effectively, but together they become a powerful catalyst for the abolition of the status quo. The proletariat, as the most dehumanized class, exemplifying the worst evils of the civil society, has a greater stake in social revolution than do the other classes. Moreover, the liberation of the class on the lowest rung of the socioeconomic ladder means the liberation of everyone above, or all of mankind. But the suffering masses will remain impotent, and freedom only a dream, until the workers realize "that *man* is *the highest being for man*" and that they have "the *categorical imperative to overthrow all conditions* in which man is a degraded, enslaved, neglected, contemptible being." [8] Thus, "as philosophy finds its *material* weapons in the proletariat, the proletariat finds its *intellectual* weapons in philosophy." [9]

There was also the question as to which national proletariat was to be the leader of the coming social revolution. It is somewhat surprising that, although Marx consistently talked in terms of humanity's interests and the emancipation of man—any man and all men—he nevertheless assigned the greatest responsibility to a proletariat that appeared to be least equipped to lead a successful revolution. Marx readily conceded that Germany was far behind Britain and France in its economic and political development. Yet at the same time he argued that Germany's economic and political backwardness, far from impeding its revolutionary potential, actually increased it. What his native country lacked economically and politically, it more than made up in philosophical sophistication. Unlike Britain and France, Germany had already formulated a revolutionary theory, and the only question was whether it could be "actualized" in a backward society lacking a revolutionary tradition. Marx's answer was an unequivocal yes. What is even more surprising, he regarded Germany's backwardness as a definite asset. In Germany, in contrast to Britain and France, society had not yet experienced economic and social stratification caused by the modern division of labor and, therefore, had failed to produce a well-defined class structure. The result was a considerable confusion concerning the historical roles of various classes and an excellent opportunity for the newest class, the proletariat, to move into the power vacuum and exploit it in the interests of social revolution.[10] Moreover, Marx implied that the absence of political sophistication and revolutionary experience would enable his countrymen to avoid the French errors of excessive emphasis on political action and change.[11]

Thus, according to the young Marx, the emerging German proletariat offered the best combination for a successful social revolution: the living proof of the evils of civil society; the freedom of action unhindered by past mistakes, present institutions, and timeless illusions; and the correct revolutionary philosophy. In the Silesian weavers' revolt he professed to see the beginnings of the future revolution, or at least concrete evidence to support his contention that the still very young and small German proletariat was already displaying the kind of social consciousness absent from the British and French workers' uprisings.[12] The view that German workers possessed greater revolutionary potential than their British and French counterparts survived until Marx's death. This is, of course, not to deny that he was frequently disillusioned with his countrymen and occasionally subjected them to bitter criticism. Also, it should be noted that despite his great confidence in the German proletariat, Marx, as early as 1844, considered the

French as most likely to provide the initial spark for the world-wide revolution: "When all the inner conditions are fulfilled," he wrote during the winter of 1843–44, "the *day of German resurrection* will be announced by the *crowing of the French rooster*." [13] This view, too, generally survived until the very end. Apparently, even as rabid a German nationalist as Marx had to make some concessions to the undeniable French revolutionary tradition.

In January, 1845, the French government finally gave in to the pressure of the Berlin authorities and ordered the expulsion of Marx and several other exiles who were known for their vociferous opposition to the Prussian monarchy. When on February 3 he left France to begin a new exile in Brussels, his revolutionary theory could be summed up as follows: the call for a social revolution in Germany, ignited by a spark from Paris and subsequently spreading to other countries, carried out by the proletariat under the guidance of a philosophy of social humanism.

III   The Communist Manifesto

The beginning of the Belgian exile coincided with Marx's growing involvement in a number of Western European dissident movements, the beginning of a close collaboration with Engels, and advocacy of a joint action with the democrats. Although Marx never modified his original notion of the proletariat's historical mission, he and Engels were realistic enough to conclude that in the mid-1840s the workers lacked the numerical strength and intellectual leadership to implement the philosophy by themselves. Another complicating factor was the spirit of the times. During the first half of the nineteenth century, the bulk of the opposition to the established order was provided not by socialism but by social democracy. Even among the class-conscious proletarians, many considered themselves democrats rather than socialists or communists. The concept of democracy itself was generally interpreted to include not only rule by the people but also a broad social program based on the principle of governmental responsibility to secure livelihood for all citizens of the state. At this time, democracy was still being sharply differentiated from liberalism, which emphasized the rights of the individual, limited representative government, and laissez-faire economics. Not surprisingly, while the former ideology was popular among the lower classes, the latter drew support primarily from the industrial, commercial, and financial bourgeoisie.

In 1847 Marx joined the Communist League, a newly founded loose association of activist proletarians and radical intellectuals having branches in Britain, France, Belgium, and Germany. The leadership and the rank and file consisted mostly of German exiles, although a determined effort was made to give the organization a truly international character. Despite the fact that neither Marx nor Engels was among the founders or official leaders of the League, they, in what subsequently was to become a routine occurrence, quickly acquired a dominant position within it, and several months later persuaded the second congress of the new organization to entrust them with the responsibility of drafting its program. The result was their best known work, *The Communist Manifesto*.

The document, published just before the start of the 1848 revolution, reflects the confusion arising from the contradictions between Marx's materialist philosophy and his revolutionary strategy on the eve of the latter's first major practical test. It will be recalled that, by the end of 1847, Marx, having shifted his emphasis from humanism to economics and historicism, was already a confirmed historical materialist. Thus, large portions of the text are devoted to the up-to-date exposition of the new philosophical thrusts and the refutation of all heresies misusing the name of socialism or communism. The recent changes in philosophy, however, appear to have had little impact on the revolutionary strategy and tactics formulated during Marx's social humanism phase. Hence *The Communist Manifesto* calls for a proletarian victory in "the battle of democracy," instructs the faithful to "labor everywhere for the union and agreement of the democratic parties of all countries," and urges that

The Communists turn their attention chiefly to Germany, because that country is on the eve of a bourgeois revolution that is bound to be carried out under more advanced conditions of European civilization, and with a much more developed proletariat, than that of England was in the seventeenth, and of France in the eighteenth century, and because the bourgeois revolution in Germany will be but the prelude to an immediately following proletarian revolution.[14]

After this assessment of revolutionary conditions in Germany, the

German comrades are instructed to "fight with the bourgeoisie whenever it acts in a revolutionary way, against the absolute monarchy, the feudal squirearchy, and the petty bourgeoisie." [15]

Yet it would be erroneous to conclude that no modifications of the original revolutionary strategy are evident in *The Communist Manifesto*. Careful comparison with Marx's previous statements shows that the alleged weaknesses of Germany's nonproletarian classes now seem to have been replaced by the affirmation of the relative strength of its proletariat as one of the telling points for a successful social revolution in the country. Furthermore, the bourgeois revolution, hardly mentioned as an important factor in Germany's road to communism during the Paris exile, now clearly emerges as an intermediate stage between feudalism and the proletarian victory. On the other hand, the retention of the basic elements of the "German" strategy is obviously incompatible with several major assumptions of historical materialism, elaborated in the introductory parts of *The Communist Manifesto*. Here Marx and Engels present a vivid description of the modern historical process and strongly imply that a successful proletarian revolution (a term which has, by now, become interchangeable with "social revolution") is possible only after an extended period of capitalist development, in which the system's many contradictions are given sufficient time to undermine it from within.

IV   The Lessons of 1848

On April 7, 1848, Marx, accompanied by Engels and other close friends, returned to his native country. Here the revolution began early in March and seemed to be an unqualified success: every day German kings and princes were being forced to grant some new concessions to the potentially explosive population. However, it did not take Marx very long to realize that despite initial defeats the state apparatus was still safely in the hands of the established classes. Moreover, his revolutionary strategy was beginning to show major cracks in its foundation. First of all, the bourgeoisie, which with the help of the proletariat was supposed to carry out a successful revolution against the feudal monarchy, was proving to be so timid that nothing really revolutionary could be expected from that quarter. Even more serious was the German proletariat's inability to close its small ranks behind some commonly agreed-upon and fairly well-defined objectives. Instead, the workers were squandering their revolutionary energies in endless factional and ideological squabbles. Finally, the petty bourgeoisie, dismissed in *The Communist Manifesto* as a remnant of the feudal era, was exhibiting greater zeal and having more impact on political events in Germany than all the other revolutionary groups put together. As might have been expected, these unforeseen developments compelled Marx to change his strategy.

The petty-bourgeois democrats were invited to join the antifeudal front and, before long, became its leading force. According to the revised Marxist strategy, both the proletariat and the petty bourgeoisie were to prod the reluctant bourgeoisie into its own revolution. "We say to the workers and the petty bourgeoisie," Marx wrote, "rather suffer in modern bourgeois society, which by the development of industry creates the material means for the foundation of a new society which will free you all, than step backwards into an obsolete form of society." [16] Subsequently, Marx temporarily abandoned the Communist League in order to preserve the unity of the revolutionary camp. As Engels later explained, there was really no other choice. The bourgeoisie "had neither the strength nor the courage to win for itself unconditional domination in the state," while the "proletariat was still unacquainted with its own historical role." Thus, the acceptance of the "democratic banner" became a matter of course because the only other alternative was "to preach communism in a little provincial sheet and to found a tiny sect instead of a great party of action." [17] For his part, Marx, utilizing the advantages of hindsight, provided the appropriate theoretical justification of the new "democratic" strategy. "The practical revolutionary experience of 1848–1849," he revealed in an article written for the *New York Tribune*, "confirmed the reasonings of theory, which led to the conclusion that the Democracy of the petty traders must first have its turn, before the Communist working class could hope to permanently establish itself in power." [18] Whatever theoretical reasonings Marx had in mind here, they could not have possibly been those expressed in *The Communist Manifesto*.

But the new strategy did not last very long. By April, 1849, Marx and Engels finally concluded that further efforts to rid Germany of feudalism were bound to fail. The conservative reaction was rapidly regaining its lost positions everywhere in Europe, and Germany was no exception. The time was again ripe for the revision of Marxist strategy. It began with a reassessment of the political events of 1848–49. Marx felt that, even in defeat, the revolution had produced some positive developments, such as the clarification of issues, a sharpening of class antagonisms, and the realization that the bourgeois and petty-bourgeois revolutions could not immediately result in the abolition of private property and wage-labor. It also had a profound effect on Marx himself. After 1848 he was no longer as eager to rely on others to fight the proletariat's battles. Although the notion that other classes could be "used" by the workers to advance their interests was never abandoned, Marx now began to emphasize the need for separate and permanent proletarian organizations. The workers had to be prepared for a long and difficult struggle, whose outcome would be determined largely by economic developments rather than by manipulations of revolutionary strategy and tactics. In other words, he was adjusting the strategy to the imperatives of historical materialism and implying that failure to do so earlier had led to the unwarranted expectations concerning the outcome of the 1848 revolution.[19]

But before settling down to await the disintegration of capitalism from the relative safety of his London exile, Marx took one last fling at revolutionary adventurism. In the spring of 1850, believing that another European revolution was imminent, he formed an alliance with the Blanquists, a group of French revolutionaries named after their leader, Auguste Blanqui. The Blanquists' program called for an immediate seizure of state power through continuous armed uprisings perpetrated by small bands of professional conspirators. The uprisings, timed on the basis of political expediency, were to be continued until the establishment of a dictatorship of the proletariat. The success of such a revolution did not depend on economic development or the class consciousness of the masses but on the perseverance, cunning, and luck of an elite conspiratorial party. Compared to Marxist revolutionary strategies up to that time, this one was most blatantly incompatible with the theory of historical materialism. Marx abandoned it as soon as the hopes for a new revolution began to fade away.

Of more lasting value but still somewhat ambiguous within the theoretical framework of historical materialism was the *Address of the Central Committee to the Communist League*. As was the short-lived alliance with the Blanquists, the *Address*, written by Marx and Engels in March, 1850, and directed to the German branch of the resurrected Communist League, was also a symptom of Marx's lingering hopes that the Continent was again on the verge of a large-scale revolution. But unlike the Blanquist adventure, this document incorporated a number of lessons taught by the 1848 experience.

The *Address* draws a sharp distinction between the interests of the proletariat and the petty-bourgeois democrats. Although both classes were fighting the remnants of feudalism and the bourgeoisie (which, since 1848, had lost its revolutionary zeal and had sold out to the monarchy, or so Marx thought), the Communists must not forget that it was the petty bourgeoisie that now constituted the greatest threat to the aspirations of the workers. First of all, the democrats had lately emerged as the most powerful party in Germany, drawing support from numerous segments of the population. Second, the petty bourgeoisie was not interested in social revolution but only in social reform, solely designed to promote their own class interests. Thirdly, after the democratic victory they would become the defenders of the status quo and, therefore, the main obstacle to a successful proletarian revolution. To counter the petty-bourgeois threat, the *Address* advises Communists to establish separate workers' organizations; revolutionary governments alongside the official government; and proletarian guard units, armed "with rifles, muskets, cannon and munitions." At the same time, the democrats must not be allowed to solidify their position in the state. A relentless pressure should be applied on them through such methods as the incitement of public opinion "against hated individuals or public buildings," presentation of demands that could not be met, and disclosure of the ruling party's ineptness or treachery. In general, the Communists are told to keep the "revolutionary excitement" going under the democratic regime and to prepare for the final battle with the petty bourgeoisie.[20]

One of the important new elements in Marxist strategy elaborated in the *Address* is the liberation of the proletariat from demoralizing alliances with other classes. The document clearly states that, in the final analysis, the workers will have to win their own revolution and, therefore, must make the necessary preparations well in advance. It also seems to put the "gradualist" approach on a firmer-than-ever basis; whereas *The Communist Manifesto* stresses the imminence of the proletarian revolution following the bourgeois victory, the *Address* warns of the dangers associated with democratic rule and is silent on the length of its duration. On the other hand, this same *Address* is surprisingly frank on the desirability of using intimidation, violence, and terror as a means to achieve power; still sees backward Germany as the most likely battleground in the near future; and calls for continuous revolutionary action, "the revolution in permanence," until the establishment of the dictatorship of the proletariat—all notions that strongly suggest Blanquist influence.

Marx's final break with revolutionary adventurism came on September 15, 1850. Speaking before a meeting of the Central Committee of the Communist League, he delivered a bitter denunciation of Blanquism:

The minority [the pro-Blanquist minority of the Central Committee] substitutes dogmatism for the standpoint of criticism, and idealism for materialism. It treats *pure will* as the motive power of revolution instead of the actual conditions. While we say to the workers: "You have got to go through fifteen, twenty, fifty years of civil wars and national wars not merely in order to change your conditions but in order to change yourselves and become qualified for political power," you, on the contrary, tell them; "We must achieve power immediately. . . ." While we specifically point out the undeveloped nature of the German to the German workers, you flatter the national feelings and craft prejudices of the German handicraftsmen in the crudest way . . .[21]

V *The Trials of the London Exile*

In 1850, at a relatively young age of thirty-two, Marx's career as an active revolutionary came to an end, a victim of the return of economic prosperity, and, with it, political reaction, to Europe. It was also a victim of his own decision to approach politics in the future strictly within the framework of historical materialism. In the 1850s and 1860s, the strategic emphasis unmistakably shifted from sporadic insurrections growing out of political expediency or romanticized notions of the revolution to large-scale class conflicts caused by economic crises in highly developed capitalist societies; from elite conspiratorial groups engaged in clandestine operations to full-fledged class parties making utmost use of the ballot box, freedom of expression, and similar opportunities provided by various bourgeois or petty-bourgeois regimes; in short, from revolutionary adventurism to the politics of the proletarian revolution. Finally, Marx's revolutionary career was a victim of the personal hardship and isolation that characterized his life in England.

Following the defeat of the 1848 revolution, Marx had again been left with no choice but to leave Germany. After a brief stopover in Paris, he crossed the Channel and on August 26, 1849, arrived in London to begin a second exile that was to last until his death. The first decade in the British capital was especially hard. Unable or unwilling to find steady employment, Marx was forced to support his growing family (his wife, a maid, and six children, three of whom died in infancy) through occasional articles for foreign newspapers and whatever sums of money the ever-helpful Engels could afford to donate from the salary earned at his father's firm in Manchester. Marx's persistent financial problems meant that his family had to live on a day-to-day basis, uncertain whether there would be sufficient funds to pay for the next month's rent or to provide enough food for the children who were continuously ill from malnutrition during this period.

Even more important obstacles to the continuation of an active revolutionary career were the British political climate and the effects of permanent exile on Marx's spirit. Although England possessed a highly developed capitalist system and one of the few existing democratic governments, a sign that the necessary ingredients for a proletarian revolution were present, its working class was distinctly reluctant to accept the historical mission assigned to it by Marx. On the contrary, as he gradually came to realize, a typical British worker craved for respectability, preferred trade unions to political parties, supported his government's colonial policies, and tended to distrust all foreigners. Under such circumstances, the Marxist doctrine could at best appeal only to an insignificant portion of the native proletariat. In a sense, the exiles from foreign countries, including Marx, Engels, and other prominent communists, lived in a separate world in England. They had their own organizations, fought their own ideological battles (which most Englishmen failed to comprehend), tried to maintain contacts with their native countries, and generally limited their social contacts to their fellow countrymen. Yet the exiles' world was only a poor substitute for the real world of the 1840s. As time went on and the prospects for another European revolution and for eventual return to their homelands diminished, petty quarrels, personality clashes, ideological hairsplitting, and the settling of old political scores began to dominate the exiles' activities. The result was that many of them gradually drifted away from the communist movement, became hopelessly apathetic, or sought escape in other pursuits. Marx belonged to the last group. Although he never lost faith in the inevitability of the proletarian revolution, the frustrations of revolutionary politics in England were too much even for this incurable optimist and undoubtedly had much to do with his decision to resume in earnest the economic studies originally begun in Paris. From 1850 to 1864, the fiery radical of the 1848 revolution shut himself in the study rooms of the British Museum for the purpose of laying bare "the economic law of motion of modern society."

But Marx could not remain in the obscurity of the British Museum forever. Even during his years of intensive study and writing, he did not entirely isolate himself from political events in Europe, especially those in Germany. Through loyal disciples such as Wilhelm Liebknecht, Marx tried to influence the course of the rapidly growing German labor movement. These efforts at best produced only mixed results, although a significant portion of the proletariat in his native country adopted Marxism as their official ideology. But a real personal challenge and a great opportunity to return to active political life came in 1864.

VI   *The First International*

In the 1860s three international developments—the Italian *Risorgimento*, the American Civil War, and the Polish insurrection—captured the imagination of the world's radicals. Although these events were in no sense proletarian revolutions, the West European communists, socialists, and other assorted revolutionaries saw in them the same struggle for human dignity, social justice, and political freedom they had been waging at home for quite some time. The association of the dramatic events abroad with domestic efforts to improve the life of the masses reinvigorated several dormant proletarian movements and gave rise to a number of new ones. It also helped to focus attention on the potential usefulness of international action to achieve national social and political goals. The latter consideration was very much on the minds of the English and French labor leaders who on September 28, 1864, convened a meeting of European workers' representatives. The announced purpose of the London meeting was to protest the suppression of the Polish insurrection and to explore the possibilities of common action in other areas of interest to the international proletariat. Although Marx had nothing to do with the organization of this event, he was invited to attend it as a prominent representative of the German exiles in the British capital. It appears that, originally, his interest in the meeting was only that of a noncommitted observer. But Marx's attitude changed as soon as he realized that this gathering of working-class activists was making a serious effort to lay the foundations for an international organization which, in the future, might significantly help to advance the cause of the proletarian revolution in the industrialized societies of Europe.

Remembering his successes with the Communist League, Marx wasted no time in becoming the leading voice of the Working Men's International Association, the offspring of the September meeting in London. Also, again following in his own footsteps of another era, he quickly managed to have himself entrusted with the responsibility of drafting the program of the new organization. It appeared in the form of two separate documents entitled *Inaugural Address* and *General Rules*, and except for one or two paragraphs was solely the work of Marx. In contrast to the *Critique of the Hegelian Philosophy of Law*, *The Communist Manifesto*, and the *Address of the Central Committee to the Communist League*, the two tracts were primarily directed to the British proletariat and concentrated on political strategy and tactics in mature capitalist societies. The fiery revolutionary slogans and confident predictions of victory in the earlier documents were largely replaced by rather sedate comments on the evils of capitalism and repeated pleas for international solidarity. Although in *General Rules* one could still find flashes of the old rhetoric, the main theme of both documents was the preparation of the working class for the coming political battles within the capitalist system. Thus, the enactment of prolabor legislation is cited as a great practical and ideological achievement, the successful promotion of the cooperative movement as "a still greater victory of the political economy of labour over the political economy of property," [22] and the organization of workers into political parties as "indispensable to ensure the triumph of the social Revolution and of its ultimate goal: the abolition of classes." [23]

In helping to launch the Working Men's International Association, popularly known as the First International, Marx expected a long and hard struggle against the ruling classes. He assumed that its outcome would be ultimately determined by economic conditions, but he also felt that well-organized and motivated workers could significantly speed up and otherwise facilitate the historical process. Yet despite his efforts, the International could not get off the ground, and until the destruction of the Paris Commune very few people knew about its existence. The most serious failure of the organization was its inability to attract the bulk of the European proletariat, especially the unskilled laborers. Most workers either remained apathetic or preferred action on the national and local levels. These problems were compounded by persistent ideological divisions and personality clashes within the organization, Marx himself making a rather substantial contribution to the latter. Thus, while a number of national labor movements flourished during the 1860s, the International was wasting its energies in largely meaningless internal disputes.

VII The Paris Commune

The Paris Commune was established by the Parisians who had defended the capital during the Prussian siege and who, following the peace treaty with Prussia, refused to surrender their weapons and accept the jurisdiction of the rural-dominated, conservative National Assembly, located in Versailles. Throughout its brief existence (March 18 to May 28, 1871), the Commune was governed by non-Marxist socialists and radical democrats who were ideologically close to the old Jacobins.

The brutal suppression of the Paris Commune by the French bourgeois government provided the International with much-needed publicity. At first Marx was cautious in his comments on the developments in Paris. He was afraid that a premature workers' uprising and its subsequent defeat might set back the timetable for a proletarian revolution by several decades. Furthermore, his sentiments toward the Commune were tempered by the influence of Proudhonism among its leaders and skepticism about its chances for survival. But caution was quickly abandoned when the Versailles troops began the massacre of the defeated Communards. On behalf of the General Council of the International, Marx wrote a long and angry address that was subsequently published under the title of *The Civil War in France*. The document, despite its explosive rhetoric reminiscent of *The Communist Manifesto*, turned out to be not a call to arms but a brilliant, if biased, analysis of recent events in the French capital. In terms of Marxist revolutionary theory and tactics, *The Civil War in France* had very little to say aside from criticizing the Commune's leaders for failing to take more drastic action against such bourgeois institutions as the Bank of France and modifying several of the author's own previously held positions.[24] Although Marx savagely denounced the victorious bourgeoisie and passionately praised the heroism of the Communards, he refused to accept the short-lived revolutionary experiment as a model for the dictatorship of the proletariat. At best, the Commune was only "a lever for uprooting the economical foundations upon which rests the existence of classes, and therefore of class-rule."[25] Marx's later comments suggest that even this interpretation of the Commune most probably was the result of tactical necessity rather than theoretical conviction. Years after the anguished cries of the Communards had died down, the author of *The Civil War in France* felt that he could dismiss the Paris Commune as "merely the rising of a town under exceptional conditions" whose majority was "in no sense socialist, nor could it be."[26]

But whatever the theoretical implications of *The Civil War in France*, it produced instant publicity for the International. Marx's impassioned embrace of the Commune caused near panic in the European establishment, which mistook his fierce language for the organization's ability to foment Commune-type insurrections. For a while, the long-forgotten offspring of the international proletariat became the object of widely shared hopes as well as fears. But the excitement faded away as soon as people and governments discovered that neither the hopes nor the fears had much foundation in reality. The International was again relegated to the obscurity of exiles' politics, from which it never recovered. One year after the publication of *The Civil War in France*, Marx, determined to save the organization from the anarchists and other rival groups, ensured its quick and painless demise by transferring its headquarters to faraway New York.

VIII   *The German Marxist Movement*

Due to his deteriorating health, Marx was forced to curtail his literary and political activities during the last decade of his life. After the decline of the International, the politics of German socialism became his last major preoccupation. Since Marx continued to reside in London, this was a poor substitute for the more exciting and challenging roles of the past. But now it all made little difference because his increasingly numerous and severe illnesses would have ruled out a more direct and active involvement anyway.

In the mid-1870s, the two largest factions of German socialism, the Marxist Eisenachers (so named after a town, Eisenach, in which this faction was founded) led by Wilhelm Liebknecht and August Bebel and the General Association of German Workers, a less ideological labor movement founded by Ferdinand Lassalle, finally agreed to bury their differences and merge into one organization, the Social Democratic Party of Germany. The Lassalleans, as the General Association was popularly known, for a long time retained the imprint of their colorful leader, who professed to be a follower of Marx and Engels but was actually much too independent, ambitious, or opportunistic to follow anyone, especially a stern and tactless taskmaster such as Marx. Lassalle was also more interested in concrete accomplishments than in ideology, an attitude that led to his collaboration with Bismarck. It is not surprising that such personality traits and political tactics eventually incurred the lasting wrath of Marx, who refused to forgive or forget Lassalle's sins long after he died in a senseless duel in 1864. Marx's intransigence toward Lassalle and his program was one of the factors that had delayed the unification of the rival socialist factions in Germany.

On the eve of the 1875 Gotha Congress, which approved the merger of the Eisenachers and the General Association, Marx was asked to comment on the proposed program for a united socialist movement. The document had been written by Liebknecht, a disciple of Marx who had become an adopted member of his family during the early years of the London exile. Ordinarily, the old man should have been more than satisfied to have one of his most trusted junior colleagues assume such an important role. But these were not ordinary circumstances. To ensure smooth sailing, the planning for the unity congress and the drafting of the new program was carried out without Marx's or Engels's knowledge. Realizing that a successful merger could not be achieved without concessions on both sides, Liebknecht prepared a draft that incorporated a number of Lassallean ideas, such as the celebrated iron law of wages. As was to be expected, Marx was upset not only about the content of the draft but also about the manner in which it saw the light of the day. His response, subsequently published as *Critique of the Gotha Program*, was unduly harsh, petty, and unfair. It also helped to dispel the notion that, after the bloody suppression of the Paris Commune, he had abandoned the revolutionary road to power in favor of conventional politics within existing capitalist institutions, especially those of the democratic variety. This notion acquired considerable credence after Marx, addressing the Hague Congress of the International, made the following statement: "But we have never said that the means to arrive at these ends [conquest of political power] were identical. We know the allowance that must be made for the institutions, manners and traditions of different countries. We do not deny that there exist countries like America, England, and, if I knew your institutions better, I would add Holland, where the workers may be able to attain their ends by peaceful means." 27

In the entire text of the *Critique*, one cannot find a single favorable phrase about the Gotha program's democratic content. Instead, it is ridiculed as containing "nothing beyond the old democratic litany," and as being "a mere echo of the bourgeois People's Party!" The document also reaffirms the conventional Marxist view of the state as an instrument of the ruling class, refers to the democratic republic as the "last stage of bourgeois society" where the class struggle will be "fought out to conclusion," and describes the transition period from capitalism to communism as "revolutionary transformation" in which "the state can be nothing but *the revolutionary dictatorship of the proletariat.*" 28

Even more revealing is Marx's and Engels's "circular letter" of September, 1879, in which they attack "the path of legality" advocated by the socialist revisionists and urge the leaders of the Social Democratic party to retain proletarian revolution as one of the party's principal objectives. The letter ends on a personal note: "As for ourselves," wrote the founders of modern communism, "in view of our whole past there is only one path open to us. For almost forty years we have stressed class struggle as the immediate driving force of history, and in particular the class struggle between the bourgeoisie and the proletariat as the great lever of the modern social revolution; it is, therefore, impossible for us to cooperate with people who wish to expunge this class struggle from the movement." [29]

Two years before his death, Marx once more restated his revolutionary strategy. In one of his last important pronouncements, he declared that revolutions which anticipate rather than reflect economic conditions are bound to fail. The Paris Commune was such a revolution, and it failed. The workers must always remember that a socialist government can be successful only under conditions that will enable it to intimidate "the mass of the bourgeoisie" in order to gain sufficient time "for lasting action." [30] Needless to say, Marx himself had many times violated this maxim. As was previously pointed out, anticipation won over reflection in 1848, 1850, and to some extent in 1871, although in the last case there is considerable evidence that the temporary alliance with the Paris Commune was primarily a tactical move. But at the end of his revolutionary career, Marx for the first time in a long while could afford the luxury of statements uninhibited by the pressures of political events in which he himself was directly involved. Consequently, in his last bit of advice to European socialists, Marx cautions them not to fall for "the doctrinaire and necessarily fantastic anticipations of the programme of action for a revolution of the future," which will "only divert us from the struggle of the present," and suggests that they allow developing economic conditions to determine the timing and specific tactics of the coming proletarian revolution. [31]

CHAPTER 5

Art and Literature in Marx's Philosophy

I The Role of the Production Process

MARX'S theoretical views on literature, the arts, and other aesthetic endeavors of man form an integral part of his general philosophy. He regarded man as a product of his material environment, which alone provides the ultimate clues to an understanding of human nature. This view was dramatically summed up by Engels in a speech delivered at Marx's funeral: "Marx discovered the law of development of human history: the simple fact, hitherto concealed by an overgrowth of ideology, that mankind must first of all eat, drink, have shelter and clothing, before it can pursue politics, science, art, religion, etc." [1]

In *The German Ideology*, Marx and Engels explained that in order to subsist man has to produce. This means that his evolution becomes closely connected with the development of production. As the productive process advances, so does man's dependence on it. The emergence of the division of labor, private property, and classes reflects the fact that the mode of production had acquired a decisive influence in human relations. Its immediate impact is seen in the productive relations, or the economic structure—"the real foundation of society"—which, in turn, determines the ideological superstructure consisting of noneconomic social institutions and a corresponding framework of ethical, philosophical, and aesthetic ideas. [2]

Thus, the true explanation of man's intellectual life is to be found in his material surroundings, specifically, in the production process. Ideas and ideological systems have no independent existence or history because "men developing their material production and their intercourse, alter, along with this, their real existence, their thinking and the products of their thinking." [3] As the mode of material production undergoes historical changes, so does the intellectual production.

To study the connection between intellectual and material production, it is necessary, above all, to deal with the latter not as a general category but in a definite historical form. Thus, for example, the kind of intellectual production corresponding to capitalist methods of production is different from that corresponding to medieval methods of production. If material production itself is not grasped in its specific historical form, it is impossible to understand the concrete nature of the intellectual production corresponding to it and the interplay of both factors.[4]

II *Art and Literature as Class Instruments*

Neither Marx nor Engels ever elaborated systematically on the exact relationship between different modes of production and their intellectual counterparts. But from the numerous short comments, scattered throughout their works, one can piece together a general picture about the nature of this relationship. Social classes appear to be the key element in this picture. It will be recalled that, in societies where the division of labor and private property already exist, there are two major classes, the dominant, or the property-owning and exploiting, and the oppressed, or the propertyless and exploited one. The dominant class controls the production process and, through it, the prevalent ideas of the period: "The ideas of the ruling class are in every epoch the ruling ideas. . . . The individuals composing the ruling class possess, among other things, consciousness, and therefore think. In so far, therefore, as they rule as a class . . . they . . . rule also as thinkers, as producers of ideas, and regulate the production and distribution of the ideas of their age. . . ."[5]

In fact, the dominant class is the only class in society that has the opportunity to assume control over the social, political, ethical, and aesthetic spheres of human behavior. It is wealthy and free from the necessity to work; and, therefore, it alone can afford activities unrelated to the struggle for subsistence.[6] The monopoly on participation in matters outside the production process puts the dominant class in a highly advantageous position with regard to its opponents. It is virtually free to advance its own interests at the expense of others. This the dominant class does by promoting only those institutions and ideas that strengthen its hold over the rest of society. For example, during the feudal era the concepts of honor and loyalty expressed the interests of the ruling aristocracy because its economic power had to be justified in terms of hereditary rights and obligations. When the bourgeoisie came to power, it introduced the concepts of freedom and equality, which were useful in opposing the remnants of feudalism and were convenient arguments in behalf of laissez-faire economics. Moreover, the dominant classes are in the habit of presenting their leading ideas as universally valid and representing the interests of all—in other words, as "eternal truths." [7]

Within the ruling class, there is a segment of intellectuals who earn their livelihood by promoting class ideology, or by perfecting "the illusion of the class about itself." [8] These purveyors of class ideas occasionally come into conflict with the "active" members of their class—that is, those who control and manage the production process—but not for very long. If the interests of the entire class are threatened, the two groups invariably reconcile their differences, thereby proving that no genuine conflict had ever existed. One can only guess that the thesis about unreal conflicts within the dominant class was advanced by Marx and Engels in order to make their monolithic class-structure theory more credible in the light of considerable evidence that most creative intellectuals are highly individualistic souls and do not easily fit class stereotypes.

Marx included writers and artists in the category of class-serving intellectuals. He also suggested that theirs is the type of commitment that goes beyond material rewards earned for services rendered to the ruling class. Referring to the petty-bourgeois writers, Marx points out: "What makes them representatives of the petty bourgeoisie is the fact that in their minds they do not exceed the limits which the latter do not exceed in life, and that they are consequently driven . . . to the same problems and solutions to which material interest and social position drive the latter practically." [9]

Even more far-reaching are Marx's and Engels's comments on the factors responsible for the development of great talents. "Raphael," for example, "was conditioned by the technical progress which the art made before him, by the organization of society and the division of labor in his locality, and finally by the division of labor in all the countries with which his own locality had relations. Whether an individual like Raphael develops his talent depends entirely upon demand which, in turn, depends upon the

division of labor. . . ."[10] In a similar vein Engels argued that
ancient Greek art was made possible only by a division of labor
based on slavery.[11]

It appears, therefore, that in Marx's class society writers and
artists are, of necessity, committed to the ruling class because
only by promoting the latter's interests can they afford the time to
develop their talents and earn a livelihood. In the process, they
acquire the ruling-class mentality and world view, which not only
color their work but also help to rationalize it. The intellectuals,
like everyone else, behave in accordance with their material interests.

III   The "Uneven Development" Doctrine

This is the main thrust of Marx's thought on aesthetics. It rejects the possibility of noncommitted literature and art in class
societies and asserts that all aesthetic endeavors are simply manifestations of prevailing material conditions. There is, however,
another Marxist doctrine on art and literature. It was presented
by Marx in a preliminary outline of his *A Contribution to the
Critique of Political Economy* and is worth quoting at length.

It is well known that certain periods of highest development of art
stand in no direct connection with the general development of society,
nor with the material basis and the skeleton structure of its organization. Witness the example of the Greeks as compared with the modern
nations or even Shakespeare. As regards certain forms of art, as, *e.g.*,
the epos [epic], it is admitted that they can never be produced in the
world-epoch-making form as soon as art as such comes into existence;
in other words, that in the domain of art certain important forms of it
are possible only at a low stage of its development. If that be true of
the mutual relations of different forms of art within the domain of art
itself, it is far less surprising that the same is true of the relation of art
as a whole to the general development of society. The difficulty lies
only in the general formulation of these contradictions. No sooner are
they specified than they are explained. Let us take for instance the
relation of Greek art and of that of Shakespeare's time to our own. It is
a well-known fact that Greek mythology was not only the arsenal of
Greek art, but also the very ground from which it sprung. Is the view
of nature and of social relations which shaped Greek imagination and
Greek [art] possible in the age of automatic machinery . . . ? All mythology masters and dominates and shapes the forces of nature in and
through the imagination; hence it disappears as soon as man gains

mastery over the forces of nature. What becomes the Goddess Fame side by side with Printing House Square? Greek art presupposes the existence of Greek mythology, *i.e.*, that nature and even the form of society are wrought up in popular fancy in an unconsciously artistic fashion. That is its material. . . . In no event [could Greek art originate] in a society which excludes any mythological explanation of nature, any mythological attitude towards it and which requires from the artist an imagination free from mythology. . . . But the difficulty is not in grasping the idea that Greek art and epos [epic] are bound up with certain forms of social development. It rather lies in understanding why they still constitute with us a source of aesthetic enjoyment and in certain respects prevail as the standard and model beyond attainment.

A man cannot become a child again unless he becomes childish. But does he not enjoy the artless ways of the child and must he not strive to reproduce its truth on a higher plane? Is not the character of every epoch revived perfectly true to nature in child nature? Why should the social childhood of mankind, where it had obtained its most beautiful development, not exert an eternal charm as an age that will never return? There are ill-bred children and precocious children. Many of the ancient nations belong to the latter class. The Greeks were normal children. The charm their art has for us does not conflict with the primitive character of the social order from which it had sprung. It is rather the product of the latter, and is rather due to the fact that the unripe social conditions under which the art arose and under which alone it could appear could never return.[12]

The significance of this statement is manifold. First, it is connected with a major theoretical work written during Marx's most intensive preoccupation with economic studies. Secondly, it deals directly and comprehensively with the relationship of art and literature to the development of the material conditions of production (there are very few such statements in Marx's and Engels's works). Thirdly, it seems to contradict the basic premises of historical materialism.

Not surprisingly, the statement lends itself to at least two different interpretations. One that comes immediately to mind is that Marx is, in effect, repudiating the deterministic relationship between economics and aesthetics summarized by him in his famous preface to *A Contribution to the Critique of Political Economy.* If there is no direct connection between the development of literature and society; if Greek art sprung from mythology rather than the prevailing mode of production; and if either

Greek art or mythology had very little to do with the then dominant class, then all talk about literature and art as mere reflections of existing material conditions, or inevitable tools of the ruling class, becomes largely irrelevant. Likewise, if modern-day capitalists and proletarians can equally enjoy Greek art, the efforts of the intellectuals who engage in "mental labor" on behalf of the bourgeoisie must frequently come to nought. After all, under this interpretation they would have to compete at least with the Greeks, who, according to Marx, represent, in certain respects, "the standard and model beyond attainment," and most probably with artists from other historical eras, such as the Roman and the Renaissance. Whether the members of the bourgeois society enjoy Greek art because it evokes the charms of childhood and is from the period that will never return, or for some other reasons, the implication that bourgeois literature and art do not possess a monopoly even on their own class seems to exclude aesthetics from the ideological superstructure.

Another interpretation of Marx's position in the preliminary outline of the *Contribution* is that its basic thesis is compatible with historical materialism. In this case, the "uneven development of art and society" doctrine is explained in terms of reverse progression. As the division of labor expands, man's intellectual creativity and output decline. In antiquity, the division of labor was still primitive and, therefore, limited in its negative effects on individual aesthetic endeavors: hence the spectacular achievements in Greek art and literature. The Renaissance economy was more advanced, but still relatively backward and not much of an obstacle to the emergence of great writers and artists. But as the capitalist era began, the situation rapidly changed. Under the modern division of labor, man for the first time in history truly became a prisoner of commodities with no time or energy for intellectual pursuits. The entire bourgeois culture is designed to train the majority of the people to act as efficient and obedient machines. Thus, it should not be surprising that the artistic and literary accomplishments of this period compare quite unfavorably with those of past epochs.

It must be conceded that there is some evidence in Marx and Engels's writings which supports this interpretation. In his most direct comment on the matter, Engels suggests that the Renaissance produced its "many-sided" heroes because they "had not yet come under the servitude of the division of labor, the restricting effects of which, with its production of one-sidedness, we so often notice in their successors." [13] For his part, Marx laments the loss of the last vestiges of intellectual creativity among the laborers under the capitalist conditions of production: "The knowledge, the judgment, and the will, which, though in ever so small a degree, are practiced by the independent peasant or craftsman . . . these faculties are now required only for the workshop as a whole. Intelligence in production expands in one direction, because it vanishes in many others." [14] Apparently, this is what Engels had in mind when he referred to the production of one-sidedness and its effects on the successors of the Renaissance era.

In another comparison with earlier socioeconomic systems, Marx somewhat sarcastically declares: "Moreover, we encounter such things as the conceit of the eighteenth-century French who poked so much fun at Lessing. They said: Since in mechanics and other fields we are like the classical Greeks, why shouldn't we also be able to write an epic? So we get the *Henriad* [Voltaire's epic poem] for the *Iliad!*" [15] In general, he paints a dark picture for aesthetic accomplishments under capitalism, whose mode of production "is hostile to certain aspects of intellectual production, such as art and poetry," [16] and under which "all the so-called higher forms of labor—intellectual, artistic, etc.—have been transformed into commodities and have thus lost their former sacredness." [17] According to Engels, the stifling impact of the capitalist division of labor is not limited to the proletariat. The exploiting class and its various subdivisions are also made subject "to the tool of their function: the empty-minded bourgeois to his own capital and his own insane craving for profits . . . ; the 'educated classes' in general . . . to their own physical and mental short-sightedness, to their stunted growth due to their narrow specialized education and their being chained for life to this specialized activity—even when this specialized activity is merely to do nothing." [18]

There are, however, very few attempts by Marx to illustrate by concrete examples the dismal state of art and literature in bourgeois societies. Whereas, in discussing capitalist economics, he supplied an enormous number of facts in support of his theoretical pronouncements, Marx's aesthetic theory is left largely unsubstantiated by factual evidence. This is all the more remarkable as it is well known that he immensely enjoyed literature and frequently expressed his views on past and contemporary writers and their works. Even the few illustrations one comes across in his writings have a rather tenuous relationship with the capitalist mode of production. A good case in point is Marx's denunciation of the "Grobian" (loutish) literature that appeared in sixteenth-century Germany. In a surprisingly bitter litany of epithets, he describes it as "stale, boastful, swaggering, conceited, offensively pretentious . . . ; arrogantly [juxtaposing] petty-bourgeois half-culture [with] popular understanding and so-called 'common sense' [with] science . . . ; thundering against reaction and reacting against progress." [19] But the only connection between this literature and the capitalist mode of production is found in the fact that it flourished during the sixteenth century, which represented the initial phase of the capitalist era. Otherwise, Marx fails to provide any information as to how the "Grobian" literature promoted the interests of the emerging middle class or how it helped to undermine the declining feudal order. As a matter of fact, it can be argued that the only purpose of these comments was to express Marx's wrath at what he regarded as an inferior, yet pretentious, literary movement. Unfortunately, such ambiguity pervades most of Marx's other statements on the relationship between the capitalist conditions of production and the works of bourgeois writers and artists.

The second interpretation of the "uneven development of art and society" doctrine, in effect, says that only under capitalism does the full weight of the productive process make itself felt upon art and literature. What are the implications of this interpretation on the fundamentals of historical materialism? There is little doubt that Marx regarded capitalism as the most oppressive and dehumanizing socioeconomic system in the history of mankind. It was also the only system of which he had considerable firsthand knowledge. The apalling poverty, exploitation, ignorance, and hopelessness around him impelled Marx to search for ways to identify and eliminate the causes of contemporary social evils. The combination of a radical theory, based primarily on current economic data, with a modern revolutionary class was presented as the only effective instrument to accomplish this task. In this sense, capitalism occupies a central position in Marx's thought and practice, so much so that, at times, one gets the impression that scientific socialism was invented for the sole purpose of rationalizing the case against capitalism and predicting its disintegration.

But Marx did not view his philosophy as merely a scientific case against the hated system. Historical materialism is a theory about man's nature, development, and future, while capitalism is just one period in his long and difficult road to freedom. An important period, to be sure, because it reflects, more decisively and dramatically than any other, the forces that have shackled the human spirit and liberty since the dawn of civilization, but still only a reflection of the universal and inexorable laws of history. These laws are the real essence of Marx's philosophy. They are predicated on the supremacy of economics over noneconomic phenomena, such as politics, ethics, and aesthetics, and their historical character precludes exceptions with regard to individual socioeconomic systems. This position was emphatically reaffirmed by Marx in his answer to the American critics who questioned the applicability of economic determinism to past systems:

> In the estimation of that paper [German language paper in the U.S.], my view that . . . the mode of production determines the character of the social, political and intellectual life . . . is very true for our own times, in which material interests preponderate, but not for the middle ages, in which Catholicism, nor for Athens and Rome, where politics, reigned supreme. . . . This much, however, is clear, that the middle ages could not live on Catholicism, nor the ancient world on politics. On the contrary, it is the mode in which they gained livelihood that explains why here politics, and there Catholicism, played the chief part. For the rest, it requires but a slight acquaintance with the history of the Roman republic, for example, to be aware that its secret history is the history of its landed property. On the other hand, Don Quixote long ago paid the penalty for wrongly imagining that knight errantry was compatible with all economic forms of society.[20]

In other words, the relationship between the economic structure and its superstructure must be essentially the same under capitalism and feudalism and during antiquity, or else Marx's laws would lose a great deal of their claim to inevitability, universality, and scientific verity.

On the other hand, Marx and Engels's insistence that the capitalist mode of production is inimical to man's creative endeavors leads one to conclude that languishing bourgeois art and literature are in a weak position to uphold the Marxist maxim that "the ideas of the ruling class are the ruling ideas in every epoch," especially since both have to compete with superior products from other eras, whose ideological content, if any, could not possibly reflect the capitalist conditions of production. Consequently, either because it assumes a close relationship between economics and aesthetics during one historical period, or because it denies such a relationship in others, the second interpretation of Marx's "uneven development of art and literature" doctrine also appears to exclude aesthetics from an active role in the ideological superstructure, thereby repudiating one of the fundamental premises of historical materialism.

IV *Art and Literature in a Communist Society*

As in the case of other social orders, the role assigned by Marx to art and literature under communism can be understood only within the context of his general philosophy. This necessitates a discussion of the conditions that precede the coming of the millennium. In societies where the division of labor is identical to private property,[21] Marx saw progressive dehumanization of man in at least three instances: excessive and forcibly imposed specialization, obsessive preoccupation with the acquisition of material goods, and the disappearance of meaningful relations with fellow men.

One of the effects of the division of labor is the assignment of each individual to a specific function, from which he cannot escape because his livelihood depends on its performance.[22] In advanced societies, most people work in factories and eventually become mere "appendages of the machines"; some are engaged in politics as lackeys of the ruling class, while still others preach a religious or secular morality that reflects contemporary social relations. Only a few are assigned artistic and literary functions, since neither requires the participation of great multitudes. Yet the results of their "mental labor" are inevitably disappointing. Like the other members of society, the artists and writers do not perform by free choice but by economic necessity. They cannot freely express themselves, their talents, and their personalities in work that has been imposed on them by others and whose product becomes an alien force antagonistic to them.[23] In pre-communist societies, therefore, the quality and the quantity of art and literature are adversely affected by an artificial limitation on the number of artists and writers and by the nature of their performance.

A second obstacle to the free development and exercise of intellectual powers lies in the compulsive desire to acquire material things. In *Economic and Philosophic Manuscripts*, Marx portrays man as a "many-sided" being who approaches life in a "many-sided" way, that is, by making full use of all the "organs of his individuality" such as "seeing, hearing, smelling, tasting, feeling, thinking, perceiving, sensing, wishing, acting, loving." The ascendance of the division of labor and private property, however, turns this versatile individual into a thoroughly materialistic moron who is interested only in things that exist as capital or can be immediatly "possessed . . . , eaten, drunk, worn, lived in, etc., in short, *used*." The many mental and physical senses of the pre-private-property man are replaced by the sense of having.[24] This "one-sided" human being, motivated solely by selfishness, represents one of Marx's images of a typical individual dominated by the division of labor. Obviously, he is not a model of great artistic and literary potential.

The third instance of man's dehumanization caused by the division of labor involves the loss of meaningful contact among individuals. In economically primitive societies, labor is a social phenomenon through which men reaffirm their social nature in the form of "self-activity" and voluntary association with other members of society. But this positive expression of human nature in labor ends when the economic progress diversifies production and divides labor into actual property, or work performed by individual laborers, and accumulated, or private, property. The accumulated property soon comes to dominate the actual labor, resulting in the separation and alienation of the productive forces (the application of labor to production by the use of skills, tools, and raw materials) from the producers, that is, the workers who supply the actual labor. The new conditions of production are instrumental in the transformation of labor from a form of self-activity and free association of individuals as individuals into a grim undertaking totally subordinated to material production. Now the only relations among human beings are material relations, or those involving labor as a necessary activity (Marx calls it "negative self-activity") to maintain subsistence. In all other respects, man becomes an isolated individual, an abstraction robbed of all "real life-content" who exists not for himself but for those who use his labor to achieve further accumulation.[25] Again, this is not an image of a man who is likely to be preoccupied with the development of his creative intellect.

As might have been anticipated, Marx and Engels predicted that the abolition of the division of labor and private property will liberate man from the slavery of material environment and enable him to regain his lost humanity. This resolution of age-old human suffering and frustration is to occur during the post-capitalist era, which they generally identified as communism. Its principal features are said to include the distribution of labor among all members of society, the reduction of individual labor time, and the creation of opportunity for everyone to pursue interests unrelated to productive labor. Marx and Engels also believed that under communism the contradiction between mental and physical labor will disappear—a development that will remove art and literature from the previously privileged status of activities in which only a few can indulge.[26] Furthermore, the elimination of the division of labor within the intellectual sphere will free the creative minds from the restrictive effects of artistic form and geographical setting. The potential Michelangelos and Goethes will no longer be limited to painting frescoes or writing lyric poetry within the physical and spiritual confines of their communities or nations: "The subordination of the artist to local and national narrowness arises entirely out of the division of labor and the subordination of the individual to a given art, making him exclusively a painter, a sculptor, etc. (the very name sufficiently expresses the narrowness of his professional development and his dependence on the division of labor). In the communist organization of society, all this disappears." As a matter of fact, art and, by implication, literature will cease to exist as professions and turn into leisurely preoccupations of virtually everyone. In the future society there will be no painters; "at most there [will be] people who, among other things, also paint."[27]

The abolition of private property will also liberate the individual from an obsession with the acquisition of material goods. Everything has been measured by personal usefulness and gain;

in the future, the guiding principle will be society's interest. The previously alienated physical and mental senses will be emancipated from the sense of having when man's object again becomes human, that is, when he reaffirms his true self as a social being. Such a man will no longer be restricted by the preoccupation with material objects and will be free to develop his heretofore suppressed capacities unrelated to material production.[28]

Another aspect of man's recapture of his social nature under communism is found in the reestablishment of labor as a "self-activity" and the freeing of human relations from the yoke of productive forces. In a society fragmented by the division of labor, productive labor turns into an alien and oppressive force that subjugates the producer. Only the elimination of private property can restore labor to its position as a means of individual self-expression and communication with others. In a communist society, productive labor will be converted into a pleasurable activity conforming to the individual producer's intellectual and physical potential and preferences.[29] This will be accomplished through shorter labor hours and a considerable rotation of social functions. No one will have an exclusive sphere of activity and everyone will have an equal chance at desired functions because under communism "society regulates the general production and thus makes it possible for me to do one thing to-day and another to-morrow, to hunt in the morning, fish in the afternoon, rear cattle in the evening, criticize after dinner . . . without ever becoming hunter, fisherman, shepherd or critic." [30] As the productive forces undergo a change from an oppressive power into a means of self-expression, the abstract, isolated individual of the past will prepare himself to join the "real community" of man in which he will rediscover "the means of cultivating his gifts in all directions." [31]

Finally, communism will also liberate man from the restrictions imposed by "localism" and nationalism. The process of internationalization, already discussed in connection with intellectual specialization, actually begins under capitalism: "In the place of old local and national seclusion . . . we have intercourse in every direction, universal interdependence of nations—and as in material, so also in intellectual production. The intellectual creations of individual nations become common property. National one-sidedness and narrowmindedness become more and more impossible, and from the numerous national and local literatures there arises a world literature." [32] But as long as private property exists, the new internationalism is utilized strictly for the purposes of exploitation. It takes a successful proletarian revolution and the socialization of the means of production to make it beneficial for all mankind. "Only then will the separate individuals be liberated from the various national and local barriers, be brought into practical connection with the material and intellectual production of the whole world and be put in a position to acquire the capacity to enjoy this all-sided production of the whole earth (the creations of man)." [33]

To Marx and Engels, the emancipated man is one who to the greatest possible extent is free of any physical and spiritual restraints on the development of his potential powers. Once productive labor begins to afford this opportunity, life becomes a continuous process of self-improvement, creativity, and enjoyment. In every human creation, whether for a social or a private purpose, the creator leaves an imprint of his personality. The product of man's work can now be said to really belong to him because in it he expresses himself. Under such conditions, professions, if understood as groups of people possessing a similar kind of knowledge or skill and practicing it to earn a living, wither away together with classes, the state, organized religion, and other by-products of the division of labor. Concomitantly, professional artists and writers are replaced by a mass of individuals who, depending on their natural talents and inclinations, devote varying degrees of time and effort to these and other aesthetic pursuits. Thus, like other intellectual phenomena with social implications, art and literature become liberated from the clutches of materialism, class content, specialization, exclusiveness, "provincialism," and turn into a part-time preoccupation for everyone.

Marx and Engels apparently had few misgivings that this amateurish approach to art and literature might result in their decline, or continued stagnation, as under capitalism. They believed that the freeing of man from his material environment would instantly release his heretofore suppressed intellectual powers, resulting in an unprecedented quantitative and qualitative progress in aesthetics. Versatility, or "many-sidedness," was the trait of the Greek and Renaissance giants who were greatly admired by the founders of historical materialism. Both blamed capitalism for the introduction of the "machine culture" in which "one-sidedness" became the watchword of the age. With the passing of private property, the causes of one-sidedness would be eliminated and the door once again would be opened—this time wider than ever, for the unhindered development of every man's "many-sided" potential. It is, therefore, quite possible that Marx and Engels modeled the image of the typical member of the communist society after their heroes of the past and expected him at least to equal, and probably to surpass, the literary and artistic achievements of the pre-capitalist man.

CHAPTER 6

The Literary Critic

I *Early Influences*

ALL of Marx's relatives, friends, and associates agreed that he immensely enjoyed reading books, and that many of them were books of fiction. Marx's love of literature was formed during the pre-university days under the informal tutelage of two individuals: his father and his father-in-law. The influence of Marx's father on his son is difficult to assess, but it most probably helped to develop in young Karl an early thirst for intellectual challenges. Heinrich Marx was one of those Jews who wanted to leave the confines of the ethnic and religious environment of his ancestors and assimilate into the culture of the country in which he lived. This, along with the desire to escape discriminatory laws, at least partially explains the conversion of the entire Marx family to the Prussian Evangelical church. But there were other reasons for this momentous step.

The elder Marx was a humanist whose outlook on life was strongly affected by the spirit of the Enlightenment. He was convinced that man is a rational being who would behave in a sensible and dignified manner if given the opportunity to do so. In Heinrich Marx these ideas of the French rationalists were combined with the belief that Prussia had effected their realization in politics. For him, the monarchy of Frederick the Great was the model of a tolerant and just rule, and if one of the great king's heirs turned out to be a scoundrel, this was a temporary aberration that had little or nothing to do with the essential soundness of state institutions. It is, therefore, not surprising that Marx's father wanted to assimilate with the people who embodied the best of two worlds: the French philosophical outlook and the Prussian political system. But for all his intellectual "boldness," Heinrich Marx was a practical and essentially cautious man who, above all, wanted his son to enter the relatively safe and profitable law profession. He was also anxious to share with the young man his views on a wide variety of subjects ranging from the notion of justice to metaphysical speculation. The philosophical discussions between father and son no doubt expanded the latter's growing intellectual interests and, perhaps, influenced his subsequent decision to abandon law as a profession. Be that as it may, the fact remains that until his death in 1838, the elder Marx was one of the few persons with whom his son had a close and rewarding intellectual relationship.

Another such individual was Karl's future father-in-law, Baron Ludwig von Westphalen, a liberal Prussian nobleman of great personal charm and highly cultivated literary and artistic tastes. He took an immediate liking to the serious young man who lived next door and was a frequent visitor to his house. Although a great difference in age existed between the two (Westphalen was already in his sixties), this did not present any problems in communication, largely because the schoolboy was very mature for his years. The old baron possessed a thorough knowledge of classical literature and could recite Homer and Shakespeare by heart, which was bound to leave a considerable impact on young Marx. Many years later, the father of modern communism recalled the friendship with the Prussian aristocrat as one of the most pleasant experiences of his life.

The local Gymnasium, a preparatory school for the university, was another factor in the formation of Marx's literary tastes. Here he received the traditional rigorous training in the classical languages and literatures that laid the foundation for future college studies. At the University of Bonn, Marx enrolled in the School of Law but many of his courses were in literature and art. He was pleased to discover that several authorities of world renown offered courses on the history of art and Greek and Roman literature and mythology, and made the most of the opportunity by attending their lectures regularly.

II *The Classics*

The youthful fascination with the literature of antiquity persisted until the end of Marx's life. This was also true of later classics, and although his general interest in aesthetics declined somewhat as the revolutionary and ideological fervor increased, he continued to enjoy good books. Among the classics, Marx particularly liked Homer, Aeschylus, Dante, Cervantes, Shakespeare, Goethe, and Balzac. According to Paul Lafargue, he read Aeschylus in the original Greek at least once a year. The themes of rebellion against the gods and service with suffering for humanity struck a responsive chord in Marx. In the preface to his doctoral dissertation, he quoted approvingly the defiant lines from *Prometheus Bound*: "I shall never exchange my fetters for slavish servility. 'Tis better to be chained to the rock than bound to the service of Zeus." [1]

Marx first became acquainted with Shakespeare during his school days and never ceased to enhance his knowledge and appreciation of the great playwright's works. Eventually, he could freely quote and identify even the minor characters from any tragedy or comedy. Once, in order to improve his English, Marx compiled all of Shakespeare's original expressions.[2] This, in part, explains the abundance of references to his plays in *Capital* and several essays. Although there are few recorded comments by Marx on the English author, his critique of Ferdinand Lassalle's drama, *Franz von Sickingen*, leaves little doubt that he regarded Shakespeare as a model playwright.[3]

Marx's knowledge of, and enthusiasm for, Goethe was as thorough and intense as that for Shakespeare, both of whom, along with Aeschylus, he identified as his favorite poets.[4] Unlike Engels, Marx withheld judgment on Goethe's personal life and politics and did not seem to be bothered by the social content, or the relative lack of it, in the poet's works. As evidenced by his own early attempts at playwriting and the quotations found in his philosophical essays of the 1840s, Marx was deeply impressed by the metaphysical dialectics of the Faust-Mephistopheles relationship.

III *Balzac and Diderot*

Among the contemporary writers, Balzac most probably had the greatest impact on Marx. Lafargue reports that Marx planned to write a critique of Balzac's *Comédie Humaine* soon after the completion of his economic studies.[5] There is some evidence that what attracted Marx to the famous novelist was the latter's realistic portrayal of socioeconomic conflicts in France during the transitional period between feudalism and capitalism. *Capital* contains several references to Balzac's works, implying that its author viewed the French writer as an authority on the economic forces that shaped the period in question and their effect on the individual members of the struggling classes.[6] It would not be too presumptuous to speculate that in the *Comédie Humaine* Marx saw a fragmentary reflection, and perhaps reaffirmation, of his theory of history. What *The Communist Manifesto* said about recent social change in supercharged ideological language, Balzac expressed in brilliant prose equaled only by a few men. As far as Marx was concerned, these considerations more than offset the fact that his favorite novelist was a staunch royalist, a dedicated Catholic, and a firm believer in the evolutionary historical progress.

The social themes of Balzac's works, however, were not the sole reason why Marx was attracted to them. After all, there were other outstanding contemporary novelists, such as Dickens or Zola, whose books also quite realistically dealt with different aspects of bourgeois society but who, nevertheless, failed to receive the same enthusiastic appreciation by him. Moreover, Marx particularly praised two of Balzac's short stories, "Melmoth Reconciled" ("Melmoth réconcilié") and "The Unknown Masterpiece" ("Le Chef d'oeuvre inconnu"), which are set in a metaphysical context.[7] In "Melmoth Reconciled," a cashier, whose extravagant living lands him in tight financial straits, sells his soul to the devil in return for unlimited power and earthly pleasures. But soon after the conclusion of the deal, he realizes that "infinite power brought Nothingness as a dowry" because now "he hungered and thirsted after things that can neither be drunk nor eaten. . . ."[8] Disillusioned and frightened, the cashier jumps at the first chance to exchange his newly acquired omnipotence for the mortal soul of a man who finds himself in a situation not dissimilar to Melmoth's own before his deal with the devil.

One can only guess why this story appealed to Marx. It is conceivable that he read into it a prediction of doom for the bourgeoisie in its mad rush to amass wealth without regard for basic human values. Balzac seems to hint at this in a reference to the French bourgeois society as "a civilization which, since 1815, has been moved by the spirit of gain rather than the principle of honor."[9] It is also possible that Marx was impressed by the author's success in combining a contemporary social message with a variation on a Faustian theme, which had fascinated him since his school days. Finally, it could not have escaped Marx's attention that the story was presented in dialectical contrasts between phenomena such as power and impotence, idealism and cynicism, emotion and intellect—a method of writing certainly close to his heart.

The second short story, "The Unknown Masterpiece," is virtually devoid of any social contact. It revolves around the dreams of an old painter named Frenhofer to perfect a method that would enable him to paint the lifelike figure of a woman. He is challenged by a young artist to compare his newly created masterpiece with the beauty of the latter's live mistress. The challenge is accepted, and the confrontation is about to take place; but when Frenhofer's canvas is unveiled it reveals only "confused masses of color and a multitude of fantastical lines that go to make a dead wall of paint." [10] The old painter realizes that his new art has failed, burns the canvas, and dies.

The reasons for Marx's unqualified admiration of the second short story are more obscure than in the case of the first one. One thing, however, is fairly clear: they could not have possibly had anything to do with his social consciousness. The impact of "The Unknown Masterpiece" on Marx was probably mostly personal. The defiant, doubting, tormented, fatalistic spirit of Frenhofer, who recklessly attacked the old and the conventional and compulsively sought to create something new, unique, and fantastic, might have easily found a sympathetic response in a man who, himself, had experienced many of the old painter's challenges, dreams, and frustrations. The fact that the tragedy of Frenhofer contains rather large doses of irony must also have appealed to Marx. When reading the story, one is not quite sure whether the author pities or mocks his hero or whether, perhaps, he does both at the same time. Balzac's ironic treatment of his personages, even those with whom he apparently sympathized, echoed Marx's own inability to tolerate individuals who took themselves too seriously. Irony, sarcasm, and irreverence were familiar traits in Marx's writings and relations with other men, as was his intense dislike of "boastful, swaggering, conceited, offensively pretentious" literature and people.[11]

Although Marx's admiration for Balzac was boundless, he listed Denis Diderot as his favorite prose writer.[12] This honor was bestowed largely because of *Rameau's Nephew* (*Le neveu de Rameau*), a short novel written in the form of a dialogue between the author and the nephew of Jean Philippe Rameau, the famous French composer. In the dialogue, Diderot represents a philosopher who has a rational outlook on life. The nephew, on the other hand, is life itself: contradictory, full of surprises, alternately beautiful and ugly, gentle and harsh, happy and sad, sincere and conceited, but always delightfully ironic. The dialectical exchanges of wisdom between the two, involving a wide range of subjects, seem to emphasize the gulf which exists between theory and practice. *Rameau's Nephew* possesses all the necessary ingredients to earn Marx's wholehearted endorsement: unobtrusive philosophical content, razor-sharp intellectual dissection of complex human problems, a dialectical method of presentation, and an unpretentious, dry, satirical style with a minimum of emotionalism and bombast.

IV   *The Patterns of Literary Preferences*

Marx's reactions to the past and contemporary classics provide us with a number of clues as to his likes and dislikes in matters of literature. He apparently enjoyed a realistic portrayal of significant social trends. But as his critique of Lassalle's drama indicates the term "realistic" did not mean a recounting of historical facts in verse or prose, or the presentation of one's favorite doctrines through psychologically unconvincing characters. To Marx, Balzac was a realist because his personages are real people caught in real problems arising from real social conflicts. Unlike Lassalle's heroes, they are historically unknown and, as a rule, not in the habit of delivering long ideological discourses reflecting the author's views. Balzac's "history" is found in the daily lives of his "nonhistorical" individuals, whose joys and sorrows, stupidity and cunning, successes and frustrations are presented in a most effective combination of literary form and social reality. That Marx immensely enjoyed such a combination is reaffirmed in his commentary on a group of well known nineteenth-century English writers:

The brilliant contemporary school of novelists in England, whose eloquent and graphic portrayals of the world have revealed more political and social truths than all the professional politicians, publicists, and moralists put together, has described every section of the middle class of "most respectable" pensioners and holders of government bonds, who look down on all kinds of business as something vulgar, down to the small shopkeepers and lawyers' clerks. How well Dickens, Thackeray, Charlotte Brontë, and Mrs. Gaskell have depicted them! [13]

But even this generalization by Marx concerning his fondness of literary realism is not entirely valid. His admiration of Shakespeare as one of the world's greatest realists, coupled with his failure to evaluate the English author's plays in terms of their social content, strongly suggests that, in this instance, the realism that so impressed Marx must have been of the purely aesthetic variety. He most certainly agreed, in principle, with Engels's observation that "in the first act of the *Merry Wives* alone, there is more life and reality than in all of German literature." [14] Vitality and earthy realism were also the principal reasons for Marx's love of Henry Fielding's novels, especially the celebrated *Tom Jones*.[15]

But again, realism, whether presented within a broader sociohistorical framework or not, was definitely not the sole criterion used by Marx in appraising literature. His reference to "Melmoth Reconciled" and "The Unknown Masterpiece" (particularly the latter) as "two little masterpieces" can be explained only in terms of such "nonrealistic" criteria as personal identification with the characters or fascination with the metaphysical context as a literary device to dramatize the treatment of such human traits as greed, ambition, conceit, and so on.[16] On the other hand, Marx's high regard for Diderot's *Rameau's Nephew* indicates that he could be profoundly impressed by a novel having an abstract intellectual content. Other writers who did not fit the realist category but were favorably received by him were Calderón, Walter Scott, Robert Burns, and the two German poets: Adelbert von Chamisso and Friedrich Rückert.[17] The literary genres represented by this group varied from majestic philosophical and religious dramas (Calderón) to romantic novels (Scott) and poetry (Chamisso and Rückert).

Marx's taste, however, was not limited to authors admired by the literary critics. His penchant for light adventure stories was well known to his family and friends. Thus, he spent many hours engrossed in the exhilarating exploits of Alexandre Dumas's Three

Musketeers and the misfortunes of his tragic Count of Monte Cristo. Marx's other favorites in this field included Paul de Kock's spicy descriptions of the seamier side of Paris and Charles Lever's novels based on life in the British military.[18]

V *Chateaubriand and Schiller*

To find out what Marx disliked in literature, one has to examine his views on Friedrich von Schiller and François Chateaubriand. The latter was subjected to bitter scorn and ridicule, and not only his literary accomplishments but his character as well were questioned. In a letter to Engels, Marx suggested that Chateaubriand, who had a fairly distinguished diplomatic career, might have accepted bribes from Tsar Alexander I, then one of the hated symbols of European reaction. As to the French writer's works, he became famous in his own country, according to Marx, simply as an embodiment of French vanity covered "in romantic dress, flaunting newly hatched expressions, false depth, Byzantine exaggeration, toying with emotions, many-colored sheen, word-painting, theatrical, sublime, in a word, a mishmash of lies, never before perpetrated in form and content." [19]

This less than flattering explanation of Chateaubriand's literary success is quite compatible with an earlier one, contained in another letter to Engels, in which Marx refers to the father of European Romanticism as "that literary aesthete who combines in most offensive fashion the elegant skepticism and Voltairianism of the eighteenth century with the elegant sentimentalism and romanticism of the nineteenth century," concluding that "stylistically, of course, this linking was bound to be the rage in France, although even in his style, despite some artistic pieces, the false often becomes apparent." [20]

Marx obviously found Chateaubriand's legitimist politics and romanticized religious views not to his liking. The writer had served the restored Bourbon kings faithfully as a diplomat, minister, and political pamphleteer. In a major work, he described Christianity as the most human religion, a great source of inspiration to defenders of liberty, poets, artists, and other romantic souls. That Marx could not tolerate such heresies is quite understandable. But in Balzac's case, Marx had shown that he could easily ignore an author's politics if he appreciated his art. It seems, therefore, that the real reasons for Marx's antagonism toward Chateaubriand and his works are to be found in the works themselves. In the two quotations from the letters to Engels, the case against the literary achievements of the famous Romantic is very vividly, if succinctly, stated. Marx loathed what he most probably sincerely regarded as entirely self-serving attempts to enhance one's literary reputation through artificially coined fancy phrases and words. Moreover, the romantic themes, so much in evidence in Chateaubriand's poetry and prose, did not sit well with Marx's *Weltanschauung* and temperament. Finally, the abundance of sentiment and the dearth of irony, satire, and wit in the Frenchman's literary output could not help but intensify Marx's dislike of him. On this last point it is interesting to note that in referring to Chateaubriand as the embodiment of French vanity, he distinguished between vanity in "romantic dress" and vanity "in a light and frivolous eighteenth-century sense," the latter presumably of the Diderot variety that Marx so thoroughly enjoyed.

The other well-known writer who, in Marx's opinion, did not deserve his literary reputation was Friedrich von Schiller. Franz Mehring, Marx's contemporary and an early interpreter of the Marxist aesthetic doctrine, firmly believes that "the gushing enthusiasm of the German Philistine for the more or less misunderstood 'idealism' of Schiller seems to have spoiled this poet for Marx from his early youth, and this 'idealism' seemed to him little more than an attempt to cloak a banal misery with high-flown phrases." [21] Engels, whose appraisal of the thematic aspects of Schiller's works Marx most certainly endorsed, called the author of *Wilhelm Tell* a purveyor of "philistine sentimental enthusiasm for unrealizable ideals." [22] But Marx's own criticism, at least that which has survived in written form, is characteristically non-ideological. In commenting on Ferdinand Lassalle's Reformation-period drama, *Franz von Sickingen*, he advised his junior colleague in the German socialist movement that one of the glaring weaknesses of his drama was too much Schillerizing, or "making individuals mere mouthpieces of the spirit of the times." [23] The historical personages in Lassalle's drama, complex and colorful in real life, are reduced to lifeless abstractions in an effort to give the play a proper sociopolitical content. Marx implied that this approach is self-defeating because a more realistic and dramatically accomplished portrayal of the characters would have increased the literary quality of the drama, as well as the reader's interest, thereby strengthening its ideological impact. Instead of Schillerizing, Lassalle should have Shakespearized.

VI *Patterns and Inconsistencies*

This sampling of Marx's known reactions to various writers and their works shows that his literary tastes did not easily lend themselves to systematic categorization. He could denounce a romantic such as Chateaubriand in the most uncomplimentary language, yet be quite enthusiastic about Walter Scott, Chamisso, and Rückert; praise Balzac for his perceptive portrayal of changing society, yet select for special commendation his two metaphysical short stories; sympathize with Aeschylus's idea of free and unconquerable human spirit, yet reject essentially the same theme in Schiller's plays as unattainable idealism. From the negative point of view, the clearly recognizable patterns in Marx's literary attitudes were his hatred of excessive sentimentality, artificially exaggerated language, and stylistic as well as thematic pretentiousness. Franzisca Kugelmann, the daughter of Marx's onetime friend and confidant Dr. Ludwig Kugelmann, wrote that "Marx had a deep hatred for sentimentality, which is but a caricature of real feeling. On occasion, he would cite Goethe's words: 'I have never had much of an opinion of sentimental people; if anything happens they are sure to prove bad comrades.' " [24] Another contemporary, Wilhelm Liebknecht, recalled in his memoirs that "as great as his [Marx's] hatred for popularity was his anger at those who sought it. He loathed fine speakers, and woe betide anyone who engaged in phrasemongering. With such people he was implacable. 'Phrasemonger' was the worst reproach he could make...." [25]

On the positive side, Marx's repeatedly expressed preferences included stylistic simplicity with a fair amount of irony and wit and thematic realism free of pedestrian tendentiousness or indoctrination. He was not, however, averse to literary probing of the mind carried out in either a realistic or a fantastic setting, especially if personal identification with the characters or the subject matter was a factor.

Marx's evident lack of consistency in evaluating literature is understandable in a man whose literary interests ranged from Paul de Kock to Aeschylus, and who refused to apply ideological criteria for this purpose. But it is quite an astonishing quality in the creator of historical materialism and its theory of aesthetics, which contends that, in any given historical period, literature merely reflects the prevailing economic conditions and expresses the interests of the dominant class. A son of middle-class parents who spent most of his adult life in a highly advanced capitalist society, a dedicated fighter and leader of the proletariat, Marx enjoyed novels, plays, and poetry representing many genres but being, for the most part, nonideological. Even where the author's ideology is discernible, as in Balzac's novels, it is unobtrusively presented, so that the literary quality is not lost in the pitfalls of polemics and propaganda. Moreover, among Marx's favorite works having an ideological flavor only a few expressed his own political or social views.

These conclusions are further substantiated by Marx's attitude toward three contemporary radical poets: Heinrich Heine, Georg Herweg, and Ferdinand Freiligrath. Marx welcomed the use of their talents in the cause of revolution and published their poems in the various journals and newspapers he edited. But when the poets' revolutionary zeal cooled off, he lost interest in them and their works. Reportedly, Marx liked Heine's satirical and lyrical verses and knew many of them by heart,[26] but displayed little enthusiasm for the more revolutionary poems of Herweg and Freiligrath.[27] This may have been partially due to the fact that Heine was a more talented writer and because Marx's personal relations with him were on the whole better than with Herwegh or Freiligrath. Be that as it may, there is no lack of evidence showing that at least in his refusal to evaluate literature strictly in terms of ideological considerations, he was fairly consistent.

Marx's essentially nonideological approach to literature probably prompted his formulation of the "uneven development of art and society" doctrine in the preliminary draft of *A Contribution to the Critique of Political Economy*. He must have been torn between the sociohistorical objectivism of his general philosophy and the individual subjectivism of his literary tastes, and the doctrine most likely represents a somewhat feeble attempt to reconcile the irreconcilable. Thus, Marx can be said to have been the first victim of unsuccessful efforts, subsequently repeated by many of his latter-day followers, to bridge the gap between Marxist aesthetic theory and practice.

CHAPTER 7

The Writer

MARX'S writings may be divided into eight major categories: poetry and other attempts at writing literature during his youth; philosophical essays; polemical tracts; political pamphlets; correspondence; speeches; newspaper articles; and scientific or economic studies. These categories are not wholly satisfactory because they tend to overlap. For example, *Capital* contains elements of poetry, philosophy, and political pamphleteering, and virtually all of Marx's works are generously endowed with personal polemics such as characterize *Herr Vogt* (to be discussed later in this chapter). But given the great versatility and the enormous volume of Marx's literary output, it seems that even a somewhat superficial classification might serve the purpose of at least identifying the major thrusts of his prolific pen.

I *Poetry*

There is some disagreement among Marx's biographers as to the significance of the poetry in his intellectual development.[1] This controversy is, in large part, due to the fact that the romantic verses written during his university days stand in such stark contrast to his subsequent economic studies. Consequently, scholars who emphasize the "scientific socialism" aspects of Marx's thought have, on the whole, dismissed the poems as youthful indiscretions that had little or no influence on his later works. Needless to say, this group represents many persons associated with the official communist establishments. On the other hand, much of the recent scholarship in the West, and some that is without official approbation in the communist East, has stressed the "nonscientific" aspects of Marxism.[2] The latter direction has, in turn, produced several subtrends, one of which focuses attention on the psychological and sociological factors in the formation of Marx's character, and their possible impact on his ideas.[3] It has also stimulated a mild interest in the poetry of his youth for its possible clues to the better understanding of this complex personality. Poetry is said to reflect man's innermost feelings, his temporary moods as well as more enduring attitudes, all of which may shed some light on the motivations behind the discernible patterns of behavior.

Marx himself admitted that his poetry was too rhetorical, but did not regard it as entirely without merit because it represented "a certain warmth of feeling and a striving for poetic fire." [4] Poetic fire there certainly was in some of his verses. Although Marx wrote several volumes of assorted poems, only two were published in his lifetime. [5] One of them, "The Player," is about a satanic violinist who plays the "dance of death" until his own demise; the other, "Nocturnal Love," sings of doomed lovers on the verge of committing suicide. Both poems are saturated with themes of frustration, defiance, and destruction. The violinist rejects God, knowing that this will destroy him; the lover repudiates his destiny by poisoning himself and his girl. There are no evident motives for these reckless acts except the satisfaction of an unruly human spirit rebelling against the conventional, predestined, oppressive world—the world with which the young Marx tried to come to grips in the loneliness, frustration, and self-pity of the first Berlin days and weeks following his departure from Bonn. The violinist's rejection of God and the lover's suicide and murder of the only person he truly loved were actually Marx's poetic assertion of his total independence from the hated world around him. He was also indirectly saying that an objective of extraordinary importance demands acts of supreme sacrifice and that a new life can come only out of the ashes of the old.

All this might be reading a little too much into the fantastic verses of a bewildered young man. Death, devils, destruction, and defiance of higher authority were common themes of the Romantic poetry that flourished at the turn of the century, which suggests that in his macabre elegies Marx was simply following somewhat dated but still contemporary trends in Western European poetry. This might very well have been the case, but it does not explain away the power and the authenticity of feeling quite evident in some of his songs of doom. Marx's poetry is, no doubt, more interesting to the biographer than to the literary critic, but its forcefulness and compulsive tension are indicative of his innate literary talents and explosive temperament, which would be unsparingly vented in his subsequent works. In this sense, "The Player" is one of Marx's better and rather typical poems:

> The player strikes up the violin,
> His blond hair falling down.
> He wears a sword at his side,
> And a wide, wrinkled gown.
>
> "O player, why playest thou so wild?
> Why the savage look in the eyes?
> Why the leaping blood, the soaring waves?
> Why tearest thou thy bow to shreds?"
>
> "I play for the sake of the thundering sea
> Crashing upon the walls of the cliffs,
> That my eyes be blinded and my heart burst
> And my soul resound in the depths of Hell."
>
> "O player, why tearest thou thy heart to shreds
> In mockery? This art was given thee
> By a shining God to elevate the mind
> Into the swelling music of the starry dance."
>
> "Look now, my blood-dark sword shall stab
> Unerringly within thy soul.
> God neither knows nor honors art.
> The hellish vapors rise and fill the brain,
>
> "Till I go mad and my heart is utterly changed.
> See this sword—the Prince of Darkness sold it to me.
> For me he beats the time and gives the signs.
> Ever more boldly I play the dance of death.
>
> "I must play darkly, I must play lightly,
> Until my heart, and my violin, burst."
>
> The player strikes up on the violin,
> His blond hair falling down.
> He wears a sword at his side,
> And a wide, wrinkled gown.[6]

Marx's unfinished poetic tragedy, *Oulanem* (written during 1836), exhibits, essentially, the same weaknesses and strengths as his poetry. The play is too discursive, lacks a well-constructed plot, and presents only superficially developed characters. Yet the tragedy has its finer moments, as in the aging poet's (Oulanem's) powerful lament of his fate and his chilling damnation of the crumbling world around him. The themes of death and damnation perhaps once more reflect a mixture of Marx's somber mood at the time and the more or less contemporary literary trends. But as in the case of the poetry, *Oulanem*, although not entirely without dramatic merit, is more interesting for its possible illumination of the author's personality than for its artistic value.

II *Philosophical Essays*

During the years 1843 and 1844, Marx wrote what have since become commonly known as his philosophical essays: the *Critique of Hegel's Philosophy of the State* (1843); *On the Jewish Question* (1843); *Toward the Critique of Hegel's Philosophy of Law: Introduction* (1843); and *Economic and Philosophic Manuscripts of 1844*. They represent a distinct phase in the development of Marx's thought and foreshadow the style of his future works. In the essays, he generally follows Feuerbach by attacking the principle of an "inverted" relationship between abstract ideas and concrete men in the Hegelian system of concepts; but he also attempts to extend the Feuerbachian critique of religion to politics and economics. During this period, Marx was still primarily interested in correcting someone else's errors rather than formulating his own theories. Thus, most of the essays are polemical and are directed against Hegel, the former Young Hegelian colleagues, and other assorted enemies of truth. But in the *Introduction*, and even more so in the *Manuscripts*, large sections are devoted to the elaboration of views which, subsequently, became the cornerstone of Marx's philosophy. Juxtaposition of the negative and the positive, or criticism and exposition, is typical of virtually all of his major works. It is difficult to say whether this represents a conscious effort on his part to practice the admired dialectical method or an unconscious manifestation of the author's combative personality, which, as was hinted at in some of the poetry, could create something new only on the ruins of the old.

Although the essays are critical of Hegel's philosophy, their abstract terminology and idealistic belief in the historical progress not only bespeak the old philosopher's continuing influence on

Marx but also, at least partially, explain the esoteric quality of their style and content. Yet there are notable exceptions, found mostly in the *Introduction*. Here Marx already exhibits the flashes of fiery eloquence in the form of repeated aphorisms, a technique that would find its epitome in *The Communist Manifesto* and other revolutionary tracts:

As philosophy finds its *material* weapons in the proletariat, the proletariat finds its *intellectual* weapons in philosophy. And once the lightning of thought has deeply struck this unsophisticated soil of the people, the *Germans* will emancipate themselves to become *men*. . . . In Germany *no* brand of bondage can be broken without every brand of bondage being broken. Always seeking *fundamentals*, Germany can only make a *fundamental* revolution. The *emancipation of the German* is the *emancipation of mankind*. The *head* of this emancipation is *philosophy*, its *heart* is the *proletariat*.[7]

Another feature of the philosophical essays that became typical of Marx's later works is his rather casual approach to organization. The largely polemical *Critique of Hegel's Philosophy of the State* and *On the Jewish Question* are developed around quotations from the works of the authors being criticized, in this case Hegel and Bruno Bauer, Marx's former Young Hegelian associate and friend. This method has the merit of directly identifying Marx's objections to certain philosophical positions, but it prevented him from systematically presenting his own views. The *Manuscripts*, and especially the *Introduction*, are more conventionally organized but, by and large, still lack the framework of explicitly stated assumptions and objectives and, most importantly, a sustained effort on the part of the writer to stay within it.[8] This relative absence of organizational cohesiveness does not, of course, mean that Marx's essays are unintelligible. It merely points to some of the difficulties that an uninitiated reader might encounter in trying to place them in the broader context of Marx's system of ideas.

Of the four essays, the longest and most important one is the *Economic and Philosophic Manuscripts of 1844*.[9] Here Marx gives economics a philosophical content in order to rationalize the abolition of contemporary human misery. Thus, such concepts as labor, property, production, consumption, and ownership are explained in terms of alienation, externalization, consciousness, and species-being; and the average industrial worker becomes an individual alienated from his labor, from labor's product, and from himself. In the *Manuscripts,* Marx seems to be saying that the causes and scope of the human plight can be identified and measured through economics, but that its full impact on men can be discovered only with the aid of philosophy. His philosophical approach to economic phenomena was not entirely abandoned even after he began to be exclusively preoccupied with economics and had adopted a new terminology to suit his new interests.

III   *Polemical Tracts*

Although most of Marx's writings contain fairly large doses of polemics, several of them are almost entirely devoted to the exposure and denunciation of the various errors and falsehoods committed by his real or presumed ideological enemies. *The Holy Family, The German Ideology, The Poverty of Philosophy,* and *Herr Vogt* belong to this category. With the exception of the last work, the content of each of these books is rather evenly balanced between heavy-handed ideological thrusts and relentless personal jabs. Collectively, they reveal as much about the author's personality as about the objects of his merciless criticism. All the books were written at least in partial response to what Marx took to be direct personal affronts to him. Thus, *The Holy Family,* a work of nearly three hundred pages of which Engels wrote some twenty-five, was a reaction to Bruno Bauer's and other Young Hegelians' attacks, published in the *Allgemeine Literatur-Zeitung,* on Marx and his views; *The German Ideology,* co-authored with Engels, was a response to several articles by Bauer and to a book by Max Stirner, *The Ego and His Own* (*Der Einzige und sein Eigentum*), in which he made numerous uncomplimentary references to communism; *The Poverty of Philosophy,* to Proudhon's refusal to cooperate with Marx and the Communist League; and *Herr Vogt,* to Karl Vogt's unprovoked smear campaign directed primarily at Marx. It appears, therefore, that Marx had sufficient ideological reasons for polemicizing against the Young Hegelians and Proudhon, and the reaction to Vogt was fully justified on purely personal grounds. Consequently, what is most interesting is not that Marx reacted but the manner in which he did.

The Holy Family, The German Ideology, and *The Poverty of*

Philosophy add up to a total of some twelve hundred pages, of which less than two hundred are devoted to the exposition of the authors' views.[10] The remaining one thousand or so pages comprise pitiless attacks on the character and writings of Marx and Engels's ideological enemies. *The Holy Family* (its full title is *The Holy Family or Critique of Critical Critique Against Bruno Bauer and Company*) was intended to demolish the Bauer brothers' (Bruno's, Edgar's, and Egbert's) notion that criticism by superior intellects would endow the masses with heretofore absent self-consciousness.[11] But within this general framework, Marx rather typically managed to touch upon a variety of topics, some of them only indirectly related to each other or to the main theme. Thus, he accused the brothers and their allies of misinterpreting Proudhon, Feuerbach, Hegel, the French Revolution, materialism, Judaism, and Eugene Sue's *The Mysteries of Paris* (*Les Mystères de Paris*). On the last subject, it took Marx nearly one hundred pages to discredit Szeliga's (the pseudonym of Franz von Zychlinski, a Prussian officer and a Young Hegelian follower of the Bauers) critique of this popular contemporary adventure novel which abounds in sociological overtones. Although the Prussian officer's article was full of pseudophilosophical allusions to the novel's nonexistent Hegelian content, it seems that the main reason for this literary overkill was Szeliga's unpardonable association with the Bauer brothers and the *Allgemeine Literatur-Zeitung*.

In most respects, *The German Ideology* and *The Poverty of Philosophy* are very similar to *The Holy Family*. They, too, are saturated with ridicule, sarcasm, philosophical hairsplitting, and a complete lack of balance between the indicated aims of the books and the literary efforts expended to achieve them. Thus, Max Stirner, one of the principal objects of Marx and Engels's attack in *The German Ideology*, is derisively called "Saint Max," "Holy Max," and "The Knight of the Sad Countenance." Proudhon, against whom *The Poverty of Philosophy* (whose title is an inversion of the French socialist's own work, *The Philosophy of Poverty*) was written, is ridiculed as early as the preface. In it, Marx sets the tone for the entire book by announcing that in France Proudhon has the right to be a bad economist because he is reputed to be a good German philosopher, while in Germany he has the right to be a bad philosopher because he is said to be a good economist. "Being both German and economist," Marx concludes, "we desire to protest against this double error." [12]

Yet, in one respect, *The German Ideology* and *The Poverty of Philosophy* are different from *The Holy Family*. Unlike it, they have considerable redeeming philosophical value. *The German Ideology* contains Marx and Engels's first systematic presentation of historical materialism; *The Poverty of Philosophy* further elaborates the new theory in many scattered paragraphs sandwiched between polemical thrusts. Moreover, the latter work was the first published Marxist text that expounds the economic interpretation of history.

Acerbic as these books are, they seem tame when compared with *Herr Vogt*. This three-hundred-page treatise in recrimination was Marx's answer to a personal attack launched against him by Karl Vogt, one of the leaders of the German democratic left and a prominent member of the Frankfurt Parliament. In 1859 Wilhelm Liebknecht, a close associate and fellow exile of Marx, sent an unsigned pamphlet to the *Augsburger Allgemeine Zeitung*. The pamphlet accused Vogt of being a paid agent of Louis Bonaparte but furnished no factual substantiation of the charge. When the paper published this material, Vogt promptly instituted a libel suit against it. He lost the case but won a great moral victory because the court proved to be blatantly prejudiced against him. But this was not the end of the story. In order to expose the man whom he wrongly believed to be behind the unsubstantiated charges, Vogt assembled all the pertinent documents introduced during the trial and published them under the title of *My Action Against the Allgemeine Zeitung* (*Mein Process gegen die Allgemeine Zeitung*). The book portrayed Marx as a ruthless egomaniac who specialized in sinister intrigues, including blackmail, to obtain money from former revolutionaries who for various reasons feared the disclosure of their revolutionary past. Ironically, up to this time Marx had not been involved in the dispute, although his contempt for Vogt and his political views was well known. But *My Action* created a sensation in Germany and, therefore, could not be ignored. Following in the footsteps of his adversary, Marx chose to seek redress in the courts. The suit was instituted against the *National-Zeitung*, a Berlin newspaper that published two long articles based on Vogt's book. Since a Prussian court was not likely to decide in favor of a man with a revolutionary reputation, the results of the trial were predictable. Marx lost the case in the first instance and twice on appeal. He was now ready to make still another appeal, this time to the court of public opinion.

In order to answer every charge, innuendo, and rumor concocted by Vogt, Marx spent a good part of the year 1860 assembling relevant information. Once he started writing, however, he did it with his customary speed, and the book was ready for the presses before the year was over. It turned out to be the most sustained and devastating personal polemic ever written by the master of this art. No stone was left unturned in exposing Vogt's treachery, baseness, and stupidity. And no phrase or epithet was spared to ridicule and discredit his views. Yet despite all this, *Herr Vogt* is more than an attack against one man. In a venomous chapter entitled "Protectors and Fellow Tramps," Marx directs his ire at the individuals and institutions that wittingly or unwittingly helped to spread Vogt's accusations. In the next chapter, he settles the score with the Prussian judicial system and the judges who threw out his case. An entire chapter is devoted to the refutation of a letter written by a former associate of Marx and published in Vogt's *My Action*. The letter characterized the founder of modern communism as being contemptuous of the masses on whose behalf he was exerting his exceptional talents and energies. One of the few sections of the book that has something to contribute besides personal invective is the one in which Marx discusses Vogt's assessment of the contemporary political situation in Europe, and in the process reveals his own views on the subject. But these few pages hardly affect the essentially negative and ideologically irrelevant character of *Herr Vogt*, which has the dubious distinction of being the only major work written by Marx that has not been reprinted or translated into a foreign language.[13] Today the book is virtually ignored by the students of Marx and his thought, except those interested in psychoanalytic studies. Even in Marx's lifetime *Herr Vogt* made a quick descent into obscurity because it failed to arouse the wrath of his enemies, and most of his friends must have agreed with Franz Mehring that, all things considered, one wished that the book had never been written.[14]

IV *Political Pamphlets*

The most important among Marx's political pamphlets are *The Communist Manifesto* (1848, coauthored by Engels); the *Address of the Central Committee to the Communist League* (1850, co-authored by Engels); *The Class Struggles in France, 1848–1850* (1850); *The Eighteenth Brumaire of Louis Bonaparte* (1852); *The Civil War in France* (1871); and *The Critique of the Gotha Program* (1875). They all relate to significant political events: the *Manifesto* was a call to the German proletariat on the eve of the 1848 revolution; the *Address* advised the same proletariat on the strategy and tactics of dealing with nonproletarian, especially democratic, parties and regimes; *Class Struggles, Eighteenth Brumaire*, and *Civil War* analyzed two revolutionary periods in Europe; and the *Critique* provided some rather caustic commentary on the unity program of the German social democracy. Some of them, the *Manifesto* and the *Critique* in particular, contain important theoretical pronouncements; others, such as the *Address*, are primarily devoted to an analysis of and to providing guidelines for revolutionary action. With the possible exception of the *Critique*, the pamphlets reflect Marx's attempts to apply the principles of historical materialism to concrete contemporary situations. In the three tracts on the French revolutions, he interprets essentially political phenomena in terms of class struggles and other socioeconomic factors. The devastating sarcasm of the tracts is reminiscent of Marx's polemical writings, but here, together with frequent outpourings of moral outrage, it provides a unique background for incisive commentary on revolutionary politics. In a typical paragraph from *Eighteenth Brumaire*, Marx explains the social content of Louis Bonaparte's rule:

This Bonaparte, who constitutes himself *chief of the lumpenproletariat*, who here alone rediscovers in mass form the interests which he personally pursues, who recognizes in this scum, offal, refuse of all classes the only class upon which he can base himself unconditionally, is the real Bonaparte, the Bonaparte *sans phrase*. An old crafty *roué*, he conceives the historical life of the nations and their performances of state as comedy in the most vulgar sense, as a masquerade where the grand costumes, words and postures merely serve to mask the pettiest knavery.[15]

In another revealing passage, this time from *Civil War*, he argues that the true nature of bourgeois civilization is reflected in the treatment of the defeated Communards:

> The civilization and justice of bourgeois order comes out in its lurid light whenever the slaves and drudges of that order rise against their masters. Then this civilization and justice stand forth as undisguised savagery and lawless revenge. Each new crisis in the class struggle between the appropriator and the producer brings out this fact more glaringly. Even the atrocities of the bourgeois in June, 1848, vanish before the ineffable infamy of 1871. The self-sacrificing heroism with which the population of Paris—men, women and children—fought for eight days after the entrance of the Versaillese, reflects as much the grandeur of their cause, as the infernal deeds of the soldiery reflect the innate spirit of that civilization of which they are mercenary vindicators. A glorious civilization, indeed, the great problem of which is how to get rid of the heaps of corpses it produced after the battle was over.[16]

In many respects, these pamphlets are the most typical of Marx's writings. In them theory is instantly verified through the analysis of current social reality; obstacles to historical progress are identified and denounced with a mixture of righteous wrath and cold logic; the leaders of the reactionary forces are subjected to the kind of personal abuse that characterizes his polemical works. This unusual blend of the theoretical and the practical, the rational and the emotional, the humorous and the somber amounts to an effective presentation of Marx's ideological positions. Some of the pamphlets aroused considerable public attention because of the political relevance, popularized theory, moralistic tone, and exhilarating attacks on established institutions and prominent personalities. But as calls to political action they invariably failed to produce the expected response. The *Manifesto* had little impact on the revolutionary events in Germany to which it was directed; the *Address* proved to be a futile gesture to revive Communist activity after the defeat of the revolution; *Civil War* gained some notoriety for the Marx-dominated Working Men's International Association but had no visible effect on the proletarian solidarity within or outside France; and the *Critique* was virtually ignored by both factions of the unified German social democracy.

The explanation for the failure of the pamphlets as instruments of propaganda and agitation can be found in their content. The *Manifesto* appealed to the German proletariat but, at the same time, denounced so many of its ideological manifestations and political movements that only a few proletarians could consider themselves qualified to accept the call. Essentially the same insistence on strict adherence to Marx's ideological positions characterizes *Civil War* and the *Critique*. Moreover, although the need for temporary alliances between the Communists and the non-proletarian classes and parties is frequently emphasized, such potential allies as the petty-bourgeois democrats and the peasants are more often than not as mercilessly attacked as the middle and upper classes. This political and ideological exclusiveness did not diminish the readability of the pamphlets, but apparently it did little to arouse the masses of Proudhonists, Lassalleans, Blanquists, Owenists, and other assorted communists, socialists, and radical democrats to revolutionary action.

V *Correspondence*

Like many intellectuals, Marx felt a constant need to share his thoughts and emotions with others. He partially accomplished this through voluminous correspondence with fellow revolutionaries, acquaintances, and relatives. Most, but by no means all, of Marx's correspondence was with Engels, who was his alter ego and a kind of social conscience.[17] His letters are important and interesting because they frequently reveal attitudes toward men and ideas that, for various reasons, could not be included in his published works. Thus Lassalle, whom Marx detested but generally refrained from attacking publicly for fear of political repercussions,[18] is lampooned as the "Jewish Nigger," [19] or an "Itzig" who "collects in his manure factory the party excrements we [Marx and Engels] dropped twenty years ago"; [20] economic studies, a subject matter to which Marx devoted most of his adult life, is referred to as "economic shit"; [21] Wilhelm Liebknecht, one of Marx's closest associates during the early years of the London exile, is called a "cow" who, in the course of a single speech, is capable of stupidity as well as cunning.[22]

But not all of Marx's letters are as colorful or abrasive. A good number of them deal with such "unexciting" subjects as party politics, philosophy, religion, art, and, above all, current events. Many letters in these categories were written to correct misunderstandings arising from faulty interpretation of the Marxist doctrine. Typical of these was Marx's letter to a Dutch socialist in which he dispelled the notion that the Paris Commune fit the Marxist model of the proletarian dictatorship.[23]

Although very few of them have survived, Marx's letters to his father are among the most interesting.[24] They reveal his attempts to find himself and to stave off the doubts, frustrations, and anxieties often encountered by young men who suddenly find themselves alone to face important decisions concerning their future. The letters also reveal Marx's self-centered attitudes and seemingly total lack of concern for the hardships of those close to him, including his father. Though these traits became even more visible later on, they did not apply to his own family, as his despondency over the death of his favorite child, Edgar, amply proves. In a moving personal confession, Marx admitted his inability to reconcile himself with the loss of his beloved son:

> Bace says that really great men have so many interests in nature and the world and so many things which occupy their attention that no loss can mean very much to them. I am afraid that I am not one of those great men. The death of my boy has shaken me deeply, and I feel the loss as keenly as though it were still only yesterday, and my poor wife has completely broken down under the blow.[25]

VI *Speeches*

Marx was a lively and persuasive talker in small informal gatherings, but he was not an impressive public speaker. His delivery suffered from a lack of natural fluency and the heavy ideological content that characterized most of his public pronouncements.[26] Moreover, it appears that only occasionally did Marx actively seek the speaker's tribune, preferring to operate in the organizational background of the various revolutionary movements with which he was associated. But there were exceptions. He liked to speak at gatherings where the audience was congenial and the atmosphere friendly. Thus, he willingly accepted invitations to address meetings commemorating significant events in the history of revolutionary workers' movements. One of his better-known speeches was delivered in 1856 at the celebration of the fourth anniversary of the Chartist publication *The People's Paper*. Except for its brevity, the tone and the content of the speech remind one of *The Communist Manifesto*. Here, too, the author mixes fiery revolutionary rhetoric with ideological arguments and ends up with an ominous warning to the enemies of the proletariat: "To revenge the misdeeds of the ruling class, there existed in the middle ages, in Germany, a secret tribunal, called 'Vehmgericht.' If a red cross was seen marked on a house, people knew that its owner was doomed by the 'Vehm.' All the houses of Europe are now marked with the mysterious red cross. History is the judge—its executioner, the proletarian." [27]

Another one of Marx's frequently cited speeches was delivered to the Dutch socialists during the Hague Congress of the First International. In it he suggested that, in the economically advanced democratic societies such as the United States, Great Britain, and Holland, the workers might acquire political power through legal means.[28] But Marx's best-known speech, *The Inaugural Address* of the Working Men's International Association, was, strictly speaking, neither a speech nor was it presented at the organization's inauguration. The address was, in fact, the political program of the association, drawn up by Marx and read by him before its general council. In the program he stressed the need for more political organization and action by the proletariat. Its general content and tone implied that the action Marx had in mind was to be essentially within the legal frameworks of individual countries. The British workers' recent parliamentary victories were extolled in the address as an example of what an organized political campaign can accomplish.

VII *Articles*

Marx's long and prolific journalistic career began in 1842 with an article on censorship written for Arnold Ruge's *Deutsche Jahrbücher*. But the journal was shut down by the Prussian Government, and the article, along with several others, was later published in Switzerland under the title of "Narratives on the Newest German Philosophy and Journalism." Subsequently, Marx edited two influential newspapers, the liberal *Rheinische Zeitung* and, in 1848–49, the democratic *Neue Rheinische Zeitung*; during the Belgian exile, he became a major force behind the procommunist *Deutsche Brüsseler Zeitung*; in England he was a regular correspondent for the *New York Tribune* and *Die Presse* (Vienna); and at various times he contributed occasional articles to the Paris *Vorwärts* and *La Réforme*, the Chartist *Northern Star* and

People's Paper, the emigré socialists' *Das Volk,* and others. It is interesting to note that Marx made very few contributions to the German socialist papers during their most vigorous organizational drives in the 1860s and 1870s. The reasons for this curious phenomenon were probably to be found in the doctrinal disputes and fierce personality clashes and, above all, in Marx's inability to participate in any socialist ventures in which he did not have a decisive voice.

Most of Marx's articles and dispatches to the mass-circulation papers, such as the *New York Tribune* and *Die Presse* dealt with current international events.[29] He wrote at length on the American Civil War, the Crimean War, Russian foreign policy, Western colonialism, British domestic politics, and so on. As might be expected, Marx's journalism was strongly opinionated and full of outrage and sarcasm directed at the callousness or stupidity of the prominent participants, usually government officials and their protégés, in the drama of contemporary politics and war. The articles, that is, the larger pieces containing background information and extensive analysis, were well researched—so much so that, at times, the enormous amount of facts results, at least by today's standards, in fairly dull reading. But many articles also included concise commentary which had the effect of reducing seemingly complex and virtually unintelligible social phenomena to a few simple and convincing explanations. In a typical article published in *Die Presse,* Marx, after a thorough analysis of the socioeconomic conditions in the mid-nineteenth-century United States, needed only one paragraph to explain the motives of the North in the Civil War:

The whole movement [the North] was and is based, as one sees, on the *slave question:* Not in the sense of whether the slaves within the existing slave states should be emancipated or not, but whether twenty million of the North should subordinate themselves any longer to an oligarchy of these three hundred thousand slaveholders; whether the vast territories of the republic should be planting-places for free states or for slavery; finally, whether the national policy of the Union should take armed propaganda of slavery in Mexico, Central and South America as its device.[30]

But not all of Marx's journalistic endeavors centered around current international developments. Articles written for small socialist periodicals before the emergence of German Social Democracy often dealt with doctrinal exposition and ideological polemics, and his contributions to the *Rheinische Zeitung and Neue Rheinische Zeitung* largely consisted of commentary on the social problems in Germany and of agitation on behalf of various radical causes. Marx's journalism, as virtually everything else written by him, was of the committed or subjective variety whose purpose was either to popularize his ideas and concrete proposals or to interpret important events in such a way as to validate the underlying assumptions of his critique of contemporary capitalist societies.

VIII *Economic Studies*

Marx's principal work on economics, *Capital*, was begun more than twenty years before its publication. In 1844 he wrote the famous *Economic and Philosophic Manuscripts*, which were supposed to be the first of several studies based on his critiques of political economy, law, morals, and politics. At that time, Marx did not realize that he would spend the rest of his life on the first, economic, study without ever finishing it. The following year he signed a contract for the publication of the *Critique of Politics and Economics*. Nothing came of this project because Marx and Engels decided first to work out the outline of their new theory of history, which they did in *The German Ideology, The Poverty of Philosophy*, and *The Communist Manifesto*. Subsequently, they were caught up in the revolutionary events of 1848 and 1849, and only after having settled down in London was Marx able to resume his critique of political economy. During the 1850s he accumulated an enormous amount of notes based on the books and documents he had read in the British Museum. This research resulted in a series of manuscripts, written during the last years of the decade, which have recently been published under the title of *Fundamentals of the Critique of Political Economy*; it also led to the publication in 1859 of a comprehensive introduction, *A Contribution to the Critique of Political Economy*, to his economic studies. However, it took almost another decade before Marx's research produced a full-fledged book. The first volume of *Capital* was published in 1867 while volumes II and III were edited by Engels after Marx's death and appeared in print in 1893 and 1894 respectively. One part of the manuscript, written by Marx between 1861 and 1863, was not included in the last two volumes because Engels intended to issue it as the fourth volume of *Capital*. But he died before accomplishing this task, and the manuscript was later published by Karl Kautsky, a leading interpreter of Marxism among the German socialists, as a separate work entitled *The Theories of Surplus Value*.

Capital is a truly unique work. It combines a theoretical interpretation of capitalist economics, an exposé of human suffering under capitalist social institutions, and an attempt at empirical verification of the author's earlier assumptions about history, human nature, and man's destiny. Much has been written about the irrelevance of its economic theories and the documentation of the various social ills in contemporary industrial societies. Outside the official communist establishments, the prevailing view today seems to be that the theories and the data were, for the most part, rendered invalid or irrelevant by subsequent socioeconomic developments. The lasting importance of this work, however, lies not in its economics or sociology but in their synthesis, or role, as a scientific reaffirmation of Marx's vision of an inevitable historical progress toward a just society in which man becomes truly free through his emancipation from the material environment.

Large portions of *Capital* consist of long excerpts from the British factory inspectors' reports, which were written in pedantic bureaucratese. But these flaws in prose are at least partially offset by the vivid portrayal of the unspeakable working conditions in Britain's manufacturing establishments during the first half of the nineteenth century. The factual reports inject life into lifeless economic statistics, lend credibility to abstract social theories, and, above all, give dramatic force to the author's indictment of the present and his predictions of the future. In a typical comment, Marx mixes moral outrage with bitter sarcasm:

We shall here merely allude to the material conditions under which factory labor is carried on. Every organ of sense is injured in an equal degree by artificial elevation of the temperature, by the dust-laden atmosphere, by the deafening noise, not to mention danger to life and limb among the thickly crowded machinery, which, with the regularity of the seasons, issues the list of the killed and wounded in the industrial battle. Economy of the social means of production, matured

[117]

and forced as in a hothouse by the factory system, is turned, in the hands of capital, into systematic robbery of what is necessary for the life of the workman while he is at work, robbery of space, light, air, and of protection to his person against the dangerous and unwholesome accompaniments of the productive process, not to mention the robbery of appliances for the comfort of the workman.[31]

Yet despite the occasional revitalizing effects of the inspectors' reports, numerous sections of *Capital* are monotonous, abstract, discursive, and characterized by mechanical recitations of endless figures and tortured arguments about economic laws of capitalism, such as the falling rate of profit. Consequently, a determined reader is continuously forced to alternate between the excitement and tension of a morality play and the melancholy of a badly written textbook.

Perhaps because he found economics so boring,[32] Marx intended his *magnum opus* to be a work of art.[33] Volume I, which the author himself edited, suggests that he tried to achieve this through numerous quotations from Shakespeare, Goethe, Dante, and other literary giants. The plays of Shakespeare were most skillfully utilized to illustrate economic arguments and to give the book overall literary elegance. For example, in order to dramatize his denunciations of the leveling and enslaving power of money, Marx quotes at length from *Timon of Athens*:

> Gold, yellow, glittering, precious gold!
> Thus much of this, will make black white; foul, fair;
> Wrong, right; base, noble; old, young; coward, valiant.
> . . . . What this, you gods? Why, this
> Will lug your priests and servants from your sides;
> Pluck stout men's pillows from below their heads;
> This yellow slave
> Will knit and break religions; bless the accurs'd;
> Make the hoar leprosy ador'd; place thieves,
> And give them title, knee and approbation,
> With senators on the bench; this is it,
> That makes the wappen'd widow wed again:
> . . . . Come damned earth,
> Thou common whore of mankind.[34]

Marx also tries to add to the literary quality of his work by imbuing economic phenomena with supernatural powers. In the

[118]

pages of *Capital*, material objects frequently acquire a kind of independent existence and develop the power of self-perpetuation and change. Consider one of Marx's many descriptions of commodity:

> The bodily form of commodity becomes its value-form. But, mark well, that this *quid pro quo* exists in the case of any commodity B, only when some other commodity A enters into a value-relation with it, and then only within the limits of this relation. Since no commodity can stand in the relation of equivalent to itself, and thus turn its own bodily shape into the expression of its own value, every commodity is compelled to choose some other commodity for its equivalent, and to accept the use-value, that is to say, the bodily shape of that other commodity as the form of its own value.[35]

This type of prose was not likely to impress many literary critics, but the notion of commodities having lifelike characteristics must have been a novel experience for many readers. On the other hand, anyone familiar with Marx's writings will not be surprised at such attempts to invest one kind of phenomenon with the qualities of another. The concepts of the dialectic, class struggle, mode of production, and others also appear to lead separate existences and to possess extraordinary powers as movers of history, determinants of human nature, explicators of material reality, and so forth.

In terms of size and emphasis on empirical data, *Capital* differs significantly from most of Marx's works. But its style, tone, and lack of organization are quite typical of his other writings. Here, as elsewhere, the author is discursive, angry, polemical, sarcastic, biased, and fond of epigrams, aphorisms, metaphors, quotations from classics, and other literary embellishments. As far as content is concerned, the same holds true. Philosophy, economics, sociology, and politics are important substantive and methodical components in *Capital* as well as in virtually all of Marx's major articles, essays, pamphlets, and books. His approach to the study and critique of social phenomena is truly interdisciplinary and no doubt originated early in his literary career. It will be recalled that in the mid-1840s Marx was already criticizing contemporary societies on philosophical, ethical, legal, political, and economic grounds.

CHAPTER 8

Conclusion

IN the preface, I have stated that Marx aimed at nothing less than the redefinition of man's purpose and role in the world. He found the contemporary man alienated from his essentially social nature, a discovery that undoubtedly influenced his decision to investigate the causes of the appalling human conditions in nineteenth-century Western Europe. Marx's studies convinced him that the principal sources of alienation were located in the material environment or, more specifically, in the division of labor, private property, and their various offspring, such as forces and relations of production, classes, and so forth. The process of alienation began with the dawn of civilization and culminated in an advanced capitalist system in which man becomes a slave of his material environment, a mere appendage to the industrial machine, alienated from his work, the work's product, other men, and, therefore, from himself. Marx predicted that the removal of the causes of alienation would enable man again to realize his full potential through enjoyable work with a social purpose and leisurely preoccupations of his own choosing, utilization of the product of his work, and free and meaningful relations with other men. In other words, the substitution of artificial material restraints by the freedom to fulfill his promise as a human being in terms of individual talent, preference, and social objectives will signal man's return to his true self.

The society in which man regains his humanity Marx called communism. In it the man of greed, who is interested only in the acquisition of things, and the man of misery, who is condemned to the daily struggle for survival (two types that form the basis of class division in private property systems), will be replaced by the social man, that is, an altruistic man who will divide his time between the fulfillment of his social obligations and personal improvement and leisure. The new man will dispense with the state and with government because he will no longer need anyone to coerce him into his social responsibilities. They will be performed voluntarily and enthusiastically inasmuch as exertions on behalf of society simultaneously fulfill and reassert man's humanity. The social roles and functions will be determined and rewarded on the basis of individual abilities and needs. Moreover, they will be constantly rotated in order to provide a variety of opportunities and challenges for all members of society and to avoid the curse of the division of labor and all its attendant evils.

It is not surprising that in this context of universal social altruism, constant rotation of roles and functions, and abundance of leisure time, Marx left literature and other forms of aesthetic endeavor strictly to the individual initiative and purpose. Whereas in class societies literature was assigned a distinct social purpose, in the society of emancipated men it loses all social connotations whether in terms of class service or opposition, public support, professional organization or differentiation, or content whose social aspects would be largely irrelevant in a situation where outstanding social conflicts, problems, and issues are nonexistent. This much, it seems, can be deduced from Marx's utterances on the subject and the logic of his general philosophy.

Marx viewed all social institutions with great suspicion. Even the dictatorship of the proletariat, a state representing the interests of the proletarian majority, was regarded by him as inherently oppressive, and differing from previous states only in degree of oppression. This explains why he visualized the future society as free of all artificial, that is, involuntary social arrangements imposed by alien forces, a category that apparently included all conventional institutions such as state, class, religion, and so on. Since Marx never defined literature as an institution but only as a form of behavior with a potential social impact, it was not destined to disappear or "wither away" but merely lose its social character. Although he did not say so specifically, Marx clearly implied that in a society in which man regains his social nature, institutions and patterns of behavior with social implications, by definition instruments of man's alienation from himself, will no longer have any reason to exist. In the future, therefore, literature will, like fishing or bird watching, cease to be an exclusive, socially significant function of the few and become a leisurely preoccupation of everyone, expressing only individual talents, tastes, or idiosyncrasies. Literature's loss of social content, institutional association, and elitist exclusiveness, will signify that in the literary sphere man has finally been liberated from the alien forces which, in previous societies, were instrumental in depriving him of his humanity.

Marx's theoretical concepts of literature as a part-time activity of everyone in a deinstitutionalized society and as a class instrument and a full-time preoccupation of the select few appear to be in sharp conflict with his own literary practice. His critiques of past and contemporary writers leave little doubt that for Marx the author's class affiliation, politics, or even ideologically unacceptable content, were far less important than such purely aesthetic considerations as thematic experimentation, psychological credibility of the literary personages, and style. The incompatibility of the concept of literature as a class instrument and his personal preferences was most probably responsible for all the tortured arguments advanced by Marx in his efforts to establish a definite relationship between this concept and the theory of historical materialism discussed in Chapter Five.

But what about the concept of literature in a communist society? How compatible is it with Marx's personal notions of superior and inferior literature? The answers to these questions are inevitably equivocal. On the one hand, the idea that literature ought to be free of any social commitments and, by implication, should be judged solely on its aesthetic merits seems to be very much in accordance with Marx's frequently expressed views on various writers and their works. The principle of art for art's sake was certainly no anathema to him. But on the other hand, one cannot help but wonder what kind of literature could possibly emerge in a society of universal harmony, greatly expanded leisure time, and a very casual attitude toward individual aesthetic pursuits. Would Aeschyluses, Shakespeares, Goethes, and Balzacs be possible in such a society? Perhaps, but not very likely. It seems that virtually all great literary works were born out of some kind of personal or social adversity. Suffering, anxiety, fear, hatred, struggle, defeat, victory would presumably disappear, both as personal problems and social issues in a utopia characterized by voluntary cooperation and social commitment, economic well-being, and personal fulfillment. Thus, it is difficult to imagine how in this atmosphere anyone could conceive of the likes of *Prometheus Chained, Hamlet, Faust, The Human Comedy,* or even *Rameau's Nephew* and *The Unknown Masterpiece.*

Equally significant is Marx's designation of literature as a leisurely activity fit for everyone. The obvious implication here is that in the future society there will be no place for literary professionalism. First of all, the social responsibilities of individuals will take priority over personal matters and, therefore, purely literary endeavors will be possible only on a part-time basis. Second, public and private subsidies and other forms of support for writers will no longer be available. Although Marx did not specifically comment on this matter, in view of his other statements about the communist society it must be assumed that most of the royalties, if there was such a thing at all, from the published works would go into one of the two social funds: reinvestment and social services. Thirdly, in a society of amateur authors, professional writers associations and other organized efforts to improve the quality of literary output would be totally incompatible with the objectives and the spirit of the new order.

It is reasonable to conclude, therefore, that in Marx's future society the likelihood of literary renaissance was very remote. Perhaps even more significantly, the objectives, the structure, and the spirit of the envisioned social order strongly suggested that the quality, if not the quantity, of its literature would be substantially below that of the despised capitalist period. Thus, if Marx's vision of man's emancipation would have come true in his own lifetime, he, who immensely enjoyed the works of famous authors, found rewarding intellectual experience in his expert assessment of their content and style, and, apparently, drew considerable inspiration from the conflicts, dilemmas, sufferings, and victories of their fictional personages, in all probability would have found the prospect of the proliferation of writings, repeatedly denounced by him as pretentious, artificial, stale—in short, produced by "phrasemongering" amateurs devoid of any literary talent—a most unhappy aspect of the new society.

Hence Marx's two theoretical concepts of literature are decidedly out of joint with his personal views. But this, of course, was neither the first nor the last time that Marxist theory did not conform with practice. Perhaps the most glaring examples of such discrepancy are to be found in Marx's erratic politics, more often than not determined by impulsive reactions to personality clashes, unforeseen developments, or the imperatives of expediency rather than by comprehensive, long-range plans based on dispassionate reading of the historical process. But before the gap between Marx's theory and practice is overemphasized, it must be noted that his concept of theory and its relationship to practice was, to say the least, somewhat unconventional.

To Marx, theory unrelated to practice was either an exercise in futility or a deceptive device used by individuals with ulterior motives. "The question whether human thinking can reach objective truth," he wrote, "is not a question of theory but a practical question. In practice man must prove the truth." [1] Yet, paradoxically, this very inseparability of theory and practice tends to place an additional burden on the theory to remain in strict conformity with the practice. If the validity of the theory has to be constantly proved in practice, then any discrepancies between the two must be regarded as demonstrating the theory's lack of validity. But, then, in Marxism things are never as simple as they appear at first. There are other passages in Marx's writings which suggest that he did not view the relationship between theory and practice as one-sided by decisively favoring the latter. "Theory is actualized in a people," said Marx, "only insofar as it actualizes their needs. But will the enormous discrepancy between the demands of German thought and the answers of German actuality correspond to a similar discrepancy between civil society and the state . . . ? Will theoretical needs be immediate practical needs? It is not enough that thought should seek its actualization; *actuality must strive itself toward thought* [italics supplied]." [2] It follows, then, that theory and practice must validate each other in a continuous reaffirmation of each other.

According to the Marxist dialectic (itself, as perceived by Marx, a combination of theory, or a method to unravel the mysteries of material reality, and practice, or a principle of change), theory and practice, as everything else in life, must continuously pass through different phases of development: at times complementing and, at other times contradicting each other, but in the end always resolving themselves into a synthesis, or a reaffirmation of their unity and compatibility. Although this general position allows considerable flexibility in the relationship between theory and practice—discrepancies may be conveniently explained away as temporarily reflecting "contradictory" phases of their development—it does not satisfactorily resolve the difference between Marx's literary theory and his literary practice. All available evidence indicates that Marx's personal views on literature remained basically unchanged during his adult life, and one cannot detect even the slightest hint that he might have changed them if he had survived the disintegration of capitalism. Hence it is evident that, at least as far as one component (practice) of this theory-practice relationship was concerned, there were no substantive dialectical transformations reflecting different stages of development.

Marx was convinced that the major weakness of Hegelianism and other contemporary philosophies was their irrelevance to man, his environment, and human problems in general—in short, their inability to close the gap between theory and practice. For his part, he was determined to formulate a truly "realistic" philosophy that focused on existing social problems and their not-too-distant solution, and, thereby, guaranteed his theory's constant compatibility with practice. Marx was impatient with people who thought sophisticated thoughts but were unable to transform them into concrete actions. Theory which did not lend itself to action was unrealistic *per se*, and what was unrealistic was also useless, because Marx, above all, was interested in changing the deplorable conditions in which man found himself as a result of the Industrial Revolution. "The philosophers have only *interpreted* the world in various ways," declared Marx's famous eleventh thesis on Feuerbach, "the point is, to *change* it."[3] But the emphasis on realism and activism did not mean that he was prepared to endorse all moves aimed at changing the status quo. On the contrary, Marx approved only those actions and programs which fulfilled the imperatives of his theory, whose very validity depended on the continuous reaffirmation by compatible practice.

The emphasis on the unity of theory and practice in Marxist philosophy suggests that discrepancies between the theoretical concepts of literature and Marx's own literary preferences must have caused him a lot of headache. But there is no evidence that this, in fact, was the case. Despite his personal literary interests, literature and other aesthetic pursuits occupy only a small niche in Marx's system of ideas. His attention was primarily focused on man's efforts to sustain life through the production of food, clothing, shelter, and other means vital to the achievement of that end.

All other human activities were evaluated by him only in terms of their relevance to and impact on the production process. It is, therefore, hardly surprising that Marx viewed politics—a direct manifestation of economic power in the crucial sphere of state and government affairs—or religion—a psychological reflection of man's economic alienation—as considerably more important than aesthetics, whose relationship with the mode of production he had barely established. Thus, even if Marx was aware that his own literary views were incompatible with the Marxist literary theory, (and there is very little evidence of that,) it would be easy to understand why he failed to see it as a major problem. But, on the other hand, these discrepancies between the literary theory and practice, as marginal as they may be within the general context of the Marxist philosophy, reflect on a small scale a larger problem which plagued Marx until the very end of his life. Our discussion of his theory and practice in politics has amply demonstrated that, in this area, the gap between them was at least as serious as in literature. If the scope of this book permitted, similar discrepancies in the theory-practice relationship could have been shown in other segments of Marxism, such as economics or religion. Hence there is little doubt that the problems of the Marxist theory and practice in literature were not isolated instances in a marginal area but a revealing microcosm of a much larger whole.

The Marxist dialectic claims that history moves by virtue of negation, contradiction, and conflict. If this is really so, then Marx's writings can be said to have made a significant contribution to speed up the historical process. Although his interests were many and wide-ranging, Marx was essentially a social critic who sought to improve the lot of the working man in the contemporary Western societies. He attacked the existing institutions and the ruling classes in order to expose their exploitative nature and thereby to promote the growth of class consciousness among the proletariat, the class to which he assigned the historical mission to emancipate humanity through its own emancipation.

These philosophical and ideological considerations seem to have been largely responsible for the heavily polemical content and style of Marx's works. It would not be an exaggeration to say that at least ninety percent of what he wrote since his university days consisted of critiques, exposés, denunciations, and other forms of polemical thrusts aimed at philosophies, ideologies, institutions, organizations, policies, programs, actions, and individuals who, in his opinion, either represented deliberate attempts to obstruct the process of history or misguided efforts of those who simply failed to realize what was best for them. Thus, Marx attacked with almost equal fervor capitalists and non-Marxist socialists, bourgeois and proletarian parties, his personal enemies and friends, leaders of political reaction and his own revolutionary associates.

The polemical style and content of Marx's works also reflected his complex personality which, like his system of ideas, was full of contradictions. One Marx was an idealist, a man of action who was capable of absorbing great personal suffering and sacrifice in the struggle to improve the life of his fellow men. When his daughters asked what his favorite maxim was, he replied: *Nihil humanum a me alienum puto* (I regard nothing human as alien to me).[4] This was the Marx whose love and dedication to his family revealed him as a warm, sensitive, and compassionate human being. The other Marx, however, was unusually ambitious, petty, intolerant, combative, authoritarian, and vindictive. Personal slights were long remembered, political rebuffs usually repaid in kind or worse, ideological heresies not easily forgotten or forgiven. A number of incipient proletarian movements floundered, at least in part, as the result of his disruptive influence. For this Marx, the favorite virtue in man was strength; his own chief characteristic—singleness of purpose; his idea of happiness—to fight; his idea of misery—submission; and his most detested vice—servility.[5]

This combination of dialectical methodology, anti-status-quo ideology, and fierce temperament has produced prose that ranks among the best and the worst in world literature. In his most memorable passages, Marx subjects the enemies of humanity, progress, and common sense to his awesome intellectual powers, inexhaustible reservoir of moral outrage, and the chilling propensity for merciless irony and sarcasm. Here his moving epigrams invoke the forces of decency to join in the struggle against evil, his carefully selected quotations from the classics bring to life abstract philosophical arguments and impersonal statistics, and his devastating sarcasm deflates the false pride and the arrogance of his enemies. When morally enraged or personally affronted, Marx would spare no epithet, verbal trick, or twisting of logic or fact to demolish his opponents' theories, character, associations, and anything else that might weaken their effectiveness as anti-Marxist spokesmen and activists. In these moments of emotional uplift the prose, apparently reflecting his rapidly changing moods, alternates from eloquent to blunt, sarcastic, somber, angry, and threatening. The reader who experiences this supercharged atmosphere, these endless clarion calls to battle, inevitably must share with Marx his many moods, his concerns about the present, and his vision of a better future. Marx's greatness as a writer lies in his ability to evoke the sentiments of compassion on behalf of the weak, the unfortunate, and the forgotten, to articulate a powerful case against the causes of human suffering, and to remind us dramatically of man's true nature and the prospects for regaining it.

But much of what Marx wrote consisted of seemingly aimless exercises in abstract thought, philosophical hairsplitting, unabashed, occasionally bordering on paranoia, pettiness, and rather crude name-calling. These were the dominant thrusts of his many so-called major works, numbering hundreds of pages, written in a barely intelligible philosophical jargon, and without an apparent theoretical frame of reference or an elementary organizational structure. There were also the "scientific" studies which overwhelmed the reader with endless facts, figures, mathematical formulas, statistical tables, theorems, axioms, laws, and other sleep-inducing devices. Unfortunately, Marx's literary gems are, as a rule, interspersed with his less spectacular pieces of writing, so that frequently it is difficult to reach the former without being exposed to the latter.

Notes and References

Chapter One

1. Marx thought that this title would also reflect the editors' desire to attract contributors outside the German intellectual circles.

2. "Critique of Hegel's Philosophy of the State," in *Writings of the Young Marx on Philosophy and Society,* ed. and trans. Loyd D. Easton and Kurt H. Guddat (Garden City, N.Y., 1967), p. 155. Hereafter cited as *Writings of the Young Marx.*

3. *Ibid.,* p. 176.

4. *Ibid.,* p. 175.

5. *Ibid.,* pp. 173–74.

6. "On the Jewish Question," in *Writings of the Young Marx,* p. 225.

7. *Ibid.,* pp. 245–46.

8. *Ibid.,* p. 247.

9. Marx describes this development as follows: "Only when the actual, individual man has taken back into himself the abstract citizen and in his everyday life, his individual work, and his individual relationships has become a *species-being,* only when he has recognized and organized his own powers as *social* powers so that social force is no longer separated from him as political power, only then is human emancipation complete." "On the Jewish Question," p. 241.

10. "Toward the Critique of Hegel's Philosophy of Law: Introduction," in *Writings of the Young Marx,* pp. 257–58.

11. *Ibid.,* p. 257.

12. *Ibid.,* p. 263. Marx probably derived his concept of the proletariat from Lorentz von Stein, though he never acknowledged this. In 1840, Stein was sent by the Prussian government to Paris to investigate the phenomenon of communism. In a subsequently published book, *Socialism and Communism in Contemporary France* (*Sozialismus und Kommunismus des heutigen Frankreichs*), he characterizes the proletariat as a class united in the awareness of the causes of its misery and the determination to end it by a revolution against the established order.

13. "Critique of Hegel's Philosophy of the State," p. 176; "On the Jewish Question," p. 240.

14. "On the Jewish Question," pp. 245, 246, 250.

15. "Toward the Critique of Hegel's Philosophy of Law: Introduction," p. 263.

16. "Economic and Philosophic Manuscripts," in *Writings of the Young Marx,* pp. 289–93.

17. *Ibid.,* pp. 293–95, 296.

18. Besides this version of communism, Marx mentions two others, both of which he rejects. The "crude" communism of Proudhon and Fourier is unacceptable because to him the "universalizing" of private property imposes workers' conditions on everyone regardless of talent, training, and so on. So-called political communism is rejected because it signifies that the process of private property abolition has not yet been completed. "Economic and Philosophic Manuscripts," pp. 301–304.

19. Marx and Engels put it this way: "Since the abstraction of all humanity . . . is practically complete in the full-grown proletariat; since the conditions of life of the proletariat sum up all the conditions of life of society today in all their inhuman acuity; since man has lost himself in the proletariat, yet at the same time has not only gained theoretical consciousness of that loss, but through urgent, no longer disguisable, absolutely imperative *need*—that practical expression of *necessity*—is driven directly to revolt against that inhumanity; it follows that the proletariat can and must free itself. But it cannot free itself without abolishing the conditions of its own life. It cannot abolish the conditions of its own life without abolishing *all* the inhuman conditions of life of society today which are summed up in its own situation. . . . Its aim and historical action is irrevocably and obviously demonstrated in its own life situation as well as in the whole organization of bourgeois society today." *The Holy Family or Critique of Critical Critique* (Moscow, 1956), pp. 52–53.

20. *Theses on Feuerbach* was published by Engels in 1888 as an appendix to his *Ludwig Feuerbach and the End of Classical German Philosophy (Ludwig Feuerbach und der Aussgang der klassischen deutschen Philosophie).*

21. "Theses on Feuerbach," in *Writings of the Young Marx,* pp. 400–402.

Chapter Two

1. Marx and Engels wrote *The German Ideology* between November, 1845, and October, 1846. The full text of the book was not published until 1932.

2. Marx, "Preface to *A Contribution to the Critique of Political Economy,*" in Karl Marx and Frederick Engels, *Selected Works* (Moscow, 1955), I, 364. Hereafter cited as *Selected Works.*

3. *The German Ideology*, ed. R. Pascal (New York, 1947), pp. 22–23.

4. *Ibid.*, pp. 65–66.

5. *Ibid.*, pp. 66, 67.

6. *Ibid.*, pp. 67–68.

7. *Ibid.*, pp. 16–17.

8. *Ibid.*, pp. 8–9.

9. Marx and Engels, "The Communist Manifesto," in *Selected Works*, I, 38.

10. Marx, "Wage Labour and Capital," in *Selected Works*, I, 89.

11. *Ibid.*, p. 90; Marx, *The Poverty of Philosophy* (Moscow, n.d.), p. 109.

12. "The Communist Manifesto," pp. 34–35.

13. Marx classified the peasants into rich and poor: the former own land, exploit the poor, and therefore belong to the bourgeoisie; the latter class consists of small holders and agricultural laborers, is revolutionary, and forms the rural proletariat. Marx's attitudes toward the peasants were rather ambiguous, however, most likely on account of his urban background. Thus, while he recognized the revolutionary potential of some, he thought of most peasants as uncivilized brutes.

14. "Preface to *A Contribution to the Critique of Political Economy*," p. 363.

15. *Ibid.*

16. Letter to Pavel V. Annenkov, December 28, 1846, quoted in *The Poverty of Philosophy*, p. 180.

17. *The German Ideology*, p. 39.

18. For a more elaborate discussion of this problem see John Plamenatz, *Man and Society* (New York, 1963), II, 274–77.

19. For an example, see Marx, "The Eighteenth Brumaire of Louis Bonaparte," in *Selected Works*, I, 332–34.

20. *The Poverty of Philosophy*, p. 109.

21. *Anti-Dühring: Herr Eugen Dühring's Revolution in Science* (*Herrn Eugen Dühring's Umwälzung der Wissenschaft*) (Moscow, 1959), p. 368. Conceived as an answer to Dühring's theories, which were creating ideological confusion among German socialists, *Anti-Dühring* turned out to be one of Engels's major theoretical works. Written in 1877, it contains the most comprehensive and lucid presentation of dialectical and historical materialism by Engels or Marx. The latter read the manuscript, approved it, and contributed a chapter on economics.

22. Engels, "The Origin of the Family, Private Property and the State (*"Der Ursprung der Familie, des Privateigentums und des Staates"*), in *Selected Works*, II, 320–21.

23. *Ibid.*, pp. 235–40.

24. Engels, *Dialectics of Nature (Dialektik der Natur)* (New York, 1940), pp. 2–4; Engels, "Ludwig Feuerbach and the End of Classical German Philosophy," in *Selected Works*, II, 397–99.

25. "Preface to *A Contribution to the Critique of Political Economy*," p. 363.

26. "The Communist Manifesto," pp. 35–45.

27. *Capital*, ed. Frederick Engels (New York, 1967), I, 76–79; "Wage Labour and Capital," p. 90.

28. Marx, *Pre-Capitalist Economic Formations*, ed. Eric J. Hobsbawm (New York, 1965), pp. 75, 83, 97; Marx, *A Contribution to the Critique of Political Economy*, ed. Maurice Dobb (New York, 1970), p. 212; "The Origin of the Family, Private Property and the State," pp. 185–89.

29. *Capital*, III, 265–66.

30. *Ibid.*, pp. 86, 249, 250; "Wage Labour and Capital," pp. 102–105; "The Communist Manifesto," pp. 38–43.

31. Marx, "Critique of the Gotha Programme," in *Selected Works*, II, 32–33.

32. In *Anti-Dühring*, pp. 390–91, Engels gave the most detailed description of the future society found in his or Marx's writings: "With the seizing of the means of production by society, production of commodities is done away with, and simultaneously, the mastery of the product over the producer. Anarchy in social production is replaced by plan-conforming, conscious organization. The struggle for individual existence disappears. Then for the first time man, in a certain sense, is finally marked off from the rest of the animal kingdom, and emerges from mere animal conditions of existence into really human ones. The whole sphere of the conditions of life which environ man, and which have hitherto ruled man, now comes under the dominion and control of man, who for the first time becomes the real conscious lord of nature, because he has now become master of his own social organization. The laws of his own social action, hitherto standing face to face with man as laws of nature foreign to, and dominating him, will then be used with full understanding, and so mastered by him. Man's own social organization, hitherto confronting him as a necessity imposed by nature and history, now becomes the result of his own free action. The extraneous objective forces that have hitherto governed history pass under the control of man himself. Only from that time will man himself, with full consciousness, make his own history—only from that time will the social causes set in movement by him have, in the main and in a constantly growing measure, the results intended by him. It is the ascent of man from the kingdom of necessity to the kingdom of freedom."

33. Mandell M. Bober, *Karl Marx's Interpretation of History* (Cambridge, Mass., 1950), p. 277.

Chapter Three

1. *The German Ideology*, ed. R. Pascal (New York, 1947), p. 7.
2. "Preface to *A Contribution to the Critique of Political Economy*," in Karl Marx and Frederick Engels, *Selected Works* (Moscow, 1955), I, 363. Hereafter cited as *Selected Works*.
3. *Capital*, ed. Frederick Engels (New York, 1967), I, 10.
4. "The Communist Manifesto," in *Selected Works*, I, 34–35.
5. *Capital*, I, 39.
6. According to Marx, the function of money is to serve as a universal measurement of value. Money as such, however, does not contain any value; it merely reflects the quantity of that sole source of value: labor time. Thus, the price of a commodity equals the amount of labor time put into it. *Capital*, I, 94, 102.
7. *Ibid.*, pp. 235–63.
8. *Ibid.*, III, 163–64.
9. *Ibid.*, I, 509–10.
10. *Ibid.*, pp. 592, 594.
11. *Ibid.*, p. 592.
12. *Ibid.*, p. 270.
13. "The Communist Manifesto," p. 37.
14. Marx, "Wage Labour and Capital," in *Selected Works*, I, 99; *Capital*, I, 622.
15. "Wage Labour and Capital," p. 99.
16. *Ibid.*, p. 100.
17. *Capital*, I, 621–26.
18. *Ibid.*, pp. 624–25.
19. *Ibid.*, pp. 626–27.
20. *Ibid.*, pp. 629, 635.
21. *Ibid.*, pp. 632–33.
22. *Ibid.*, p. 636.
23. *Ibid.*, III, 213, 216–17.
24. *Ibid.*, p. 249; "The Communist Manifesto," pp. 37–38.
25. *Capital*, III, 232–37. Marx also lists foreign trade and the increase of stock capital as economic factors that help to slow down the falling profit rate. *Capital*, III, 237–40.
26. *Ibid.*, p. 251.
27. *Ibid.*, pp. 250–51.
28. *Ibid.*, pp. 253, 256.
29. *Ibid.*, p. 255.
30. *Ibid.*, pp. 254–60.
31. *Ibid.*, p. 259.

32. *Ibid.*, pp. 250, 257–58.

33. Besides the many crises directly associated with the falling rate of profit, Marx also devotes considerable attention to crises arising from *disproportionality* among the various capitalist lines of production and the *underconsumption* of the impoverished masses. For a comprehensive treatment of these crises, see Paul M. Sweezy's *The Theory of Capitalist Development* (New York, 1956).

34. *Capital*, I, 645.

35. *Ibid.*, p. 763.

36. "Preface to *A Contribution to the Critique of Political Economy*," p. 363.

37. *Capital*, I, 763.

Chapter Four

1. One of the poems included this stanza:

> Never can I be at peace
> For my soul is powerfully driven.
> I must strive and struggle onward
> In a restless fury of my own.

Cited in Robert Payne, *Marx* (New York, 1968), p. 61.

2. "Reflections of a Youth on Choosing an Occupation," in *Writings of the Young Marx on Philosophy and Society*, ed. and trans. Loyd D. Easton and Kurt H. Guddat (Garden City, N.Y., 1967), p. 39. Hereafter cited as *Writings of the Young Marx.*

3. "Foreword to Thesis: The Difference Between the Natural Philosophy of Democritus and the Natural Philosophy of Epicurus," in Karl Marx and Frederick Engels, *On Religion* (Moscow, 1957), p. 15.

4. "For a Ruthless Criticism of Everything Existing," in *The Marx-Engels Reader*, ed. Robert C. Tucker (New York, 1972), p. 8.

5. "Communism and the Augsburg 'Allgemeine Zeitung,'" in *Writings of the Young Marx*, pp. 131–35.

6. The last one was an article published in *Vorwärts*, a German socialist paper issued in Paris, on August 7 and 10, in 1844.

7. Marx, "Critical Notes on 'The King of Prussia and Social Reform,'" in *Writings of the Young Marx*, p. 357.

8. Marx, "Toward the Critique of Hegel's Philosophy of Law: Introduction," in *Writings of the Young Marx*, pp. 257–58.

9. *Ibid.*, p. 263.

10. *Ibid.*, pp. 261–63.

11. "Critical Notes on 'The King of Prussia and Social Reform,'" pp. 349–50.

12. *Ibid.*, pp. 352–53.

13. "Toward the Critique of Hegel's Philosophy of Law: Introduction," p. 264.

14. Marx and Engels, "The Communist Manifesto," in Karl Marx and Frederick Engels, *Selected Works* (Moscow, 1955), I, 53, 65. Hereafter cited as *Selected Works.*

15. *Ibid.,* p. 65.

16. *Neue Rheinische Zeitung* (January 21, 1849), quoted in Boris Nicolaievsky and Otto Maenchen-Helfen, *Karl Marx: Man and Fighter (Karl und Jenny Marx, ein Lebensweg)* (Philadelphia, 1936), pp. 186–87.

17. Engels, "Marx and the *Neue Rheinische Zeitung* (1848–1849)," in *Selected Works,* II, 329.

18. *New York Tribune* (December 22, 1852), in Marx, *Revolution and Counter-Revolution, or Germany in 1848,* ed. Eleanor Marx Aveling (Chicago, n.d.), p. 186.

19. Just before his death, Engels admitted that, during the initial phases of the 1848 revolution, he and Marx were too much "under the spell of previous historical experience, particularly that of France," a condition that led them erroneously to conclude that this was a social revolution that "could only end in the final victory of the proletariat." "Introduction to Karl Marx's *The Class Struggles in France, 1848 to 1850,*" in *Selected Works,* I, 122.

20. "Address of the Central Committee to the Communist League," in *Selected Works,* I, 106–17.

21. Quoted by Marx in his pamphlet, "Revelations Concerning the Communist Trial in Cologne," in Karl Marx and Frederick Engels, *Selected Correspondence, 1846–1895* (New York, 1942), p. 92. Hereafter cited as *Selected Correspondence.*

22. "Inaugural Address of the Working Men's International Association," in *Selected Works,* I, 383.

23. "General Rules of the International Working Men's Association," in *Selected Works,* I, 388.

24. In *The Civil War in France* Marx gave qualified approval to the Paris Commune's federalism, although in the *Address of the Central Committee to the Communist League* he declared that a centralized state was the most effective way to socialism. Also, in *The Civil War in France* he implicitly endorsed the Proudhonist notion that the victorious workers must immediately destroy all remnants of the bourgeois state. This view contradicted his previous position, elaborated in *The Communist Manifesto,* that the proletariat must use the bourgeois state apparatus to establish a classless society.

25. "The Civil War in France," in *Selected Works,* I, 522.

26. Letter to Domela Nieuwenhuis, February 22, 1881, in *Selected Correspondence,* p. 387.

27. Quoted in Nicolaievsky and Maenchen-Helfen, *op. cit.*, pp. 363–64.

28. "Critique of the Gotha Programme," in *Selected Works*, II, 32–33.

29. Letter to Bebel, Liebknecht, Bracke and Others, September, 1879, in *Selected Correspondence*, p. 376.

30. Letter to Domela Nieuwenhuis, February 22, 1881, in *Selected Correspondence*, p. 386.

31. *Ibid.*, p. 387.

Chapter Five

1. "Speech at the Graveside of Karl Marx," in Karl Marx and Frederick Engels, *Selected Works* (Moscow, 1955), II, 167.

2. Marx, "Preface to *A Contribution to the Critique of Political Economy*," in *Selected Works*, I, 363; Engels, *Anti-Dühring: Herr Eugen Dühring's Revolution in Science* (Moscow, 1959), pp. 41, 124–25. Hereafter cited as *Anti-Dühring*.

3. Marx and Engels, *The German Ideology*, ed. R. Pascal (New York, 1947), pp. 14–15.

4. Marx, "Theories of Surplus Value," in Karl Marx and Frederick Engels, *Literature and Art: Selections from Their Writings* (New York, 1947), p. 27. Hereafter cited as *Literature and Art*.

5. *The German Ideology*, p. 39.

6. *Ibid.*, p. 76; *Anti-Dühring*, p. 251.

7. *The German Ideology*, pp. 40–41.

8. *Ibid.*, p. 40.

9. "The Eighteenth Brumaire of Louis Bonaparte," in *Selected Works*, I, 275.

10. "The German Ideology," in *Literature and Art*, p. 75.

11. *Anti-Dühring*, p. 249.

12. "A Contribution to the Critique of Political Economy," in *Literature and Art*, pp. 18–20.

13. *Dialectics of Nature* (New York, 1963), p. 3.

14. *Capital*, ed. Frederick Engels (New York, 1967), I, 361.

15. "Theories of Surplus Value," in *Literature and Art*, p. 28.

16. *Ibid.*

17. "Arbeitslohn," quoted in Mikhail Lifshitz, *The Philosophy of Art of Karl Marx*, ed. Angel Flores (New York, 1938), p. 80.

18. *Anti-Dühring*, p. 404.

19. "Moralizing Criticism of Critical Morality," in *Literature and Art*, p. 78.

20. *Capital*, I, 82.

21. Marx and Engels described this phenomenon as follows: "Division of labor and private property are, moreover, identical expressions:

in the one the same thing is affirmed with reference to activity as is affirmed in the other with reference to the product of the activity." *The German Ideology,* p. 22.

22. *The German Ideology,* p. 22.

23. *Ibid.*

24. "Economic and Philosophic Manuscripts," in *Writings of the Young Marx on Philosophy and Society,* ed. and trans. Loyd D. Easton and Kurt H. Guddat (Garden City, N.Y., 1967), pp. 307–308. Marx develops new variations on this theme in his subsequent works; one such example is the concept of commodity fetishism, elaborated in the first volume of *Capital.*

25. *The German Ideology,* pp. 64–66.

26. *Anti-Dühring,* pp. 251; Marx, "Critique of the Gotha Programme," in *Selected Works,* II, 24.

27. "The German Ideology," in *Literature and Art,* p. 76.

28. "Economic and Philosophic Manuscripts," *op. cit.,* pp. 308–309.

29. *The German Ideology,* p. 66; "Critique of the Gotha Programme," p. 24; *Anti-Dühring,* p. 406.

30. *The German Ideology,* p. 22. Engels described this process as follows: "It is true, that to the mode of thought of the educated classes which Herr Dühring has inherited, it must seem monstrous that in time to come there will no longer be any professional porters or architects, and that the man who for half an hour gives instructions as an architect will also act as a porter for a period, until his activity as an architect is again required." *Anti-Dühring,* p. 277.

31. *The German Ideology,* pp. 74–75.

32. Marx and Engels, "The Communist Manifesto," in *Selected Works,* I, 37–38.

33. *The German Ideology,* p. 27.

Chapter Six

1. "Foreword to Thesis: The Difference Between the Natural Philosophy of Democritus and the Natural Philosophy of Epicurus," in Karl Marx and Frederick Engels, *On Religion,* (Moscow, 1957), p. 15.

2. Paul Lafargue, "Reminiscences of Marx," in *Reminiscences of Marx and Engels* (Moscow, n.d.), p. 74. Hereafter cited as *Reminiscences.*

3. Letter to Ferdinand Lassalle, April 19, 1859, in Karl Marx and Frederick Engels, *Literature and Art: Selections from Their Writings* (New York, 1947), p. 48. Hereafter cited as *Literature and Art.*

4. Laura Marx, "Confessions," in *Reminiscences,* p. 266.

5. "Reminiscences of Marx," p. 75.

6. *Capital,* ed. Frederick Engels (New York, 1967), I, 589; Letter to Engels, December 14, 1868, in *Literature and Art,* p. 135.

7. Letter to Engels, February 25, 1867, in *Literature and Art*, p. 135.

8. Honoré de Balzac, "The Magic Skin, The Quest for the Absolute and Other Stories," in *The Works of Honoré Balzac* (Philadelphia, 1901), I, 328–29.

9. *Ibid.*, p. 296.

10. *Ibid.*, p. 237.

11. "Moralizing Criticism and Critical Morality," in *Literature and Art*, p. 78.

12. Laura Marx, "Confessions," p. 266.

13. "The English Middle Class," *New York Tribune*, August 1, 1854, in *Literature and Art*, p. 133.

14. Letter to Marx, December 10, 1873, in *Literature and Art*, p. 49.

15. "Reminiscences of Marx," p. 74.

16. Letter to Engels, February 25, 1867, in *Literature and Art*, p. 135.

17. "Reminiscences of Marx," p. 74; Franzisca Kugelmann, "Small Traits of Marx's Great Character," in *Reminiscences*, p. 278.

18. "Reminiscences of Marx," p. 74; Franz Mehring, *Karl Marx: The Story of His Life (Karl Marx: Geschichte seines Lebens)* (London, 1936), pp. 504–505.

19. Letter to Engels, November 30, 1873, in *Literature and Art*, p. 133.

20. Letter to Engels, October 26, 1854, in *Literature and Art*, p. 134.

21. Mehring, *Karl Marx*, p. 503.

22. "Ludwig Feuerbach and the End of Classical German Philosophy," in Karl Marx and Frederick Engels, *Selected Works* (Moscow, 1955), II, 375.

23. Letter to Lassalle, April 19, 1859, in *Literature and Art*, p. 48.

24. "Small Traits of Marx's Great Character," p. 275.

25. Wilhelm Liebknecht, "Reminiscences of Marx," in *Reminiscenses*, pp. 101–102.

26. Lafargue, "Reminiscences of Marx," p. 74.

27. Peter Demetz, *Marx, Engels, and the Poets (Marx, Engels und die Dichter)* (Chicago, 1967), pp. 82–101.

Chapter Seven

1. See Franz Mehring, *Karl Marx: The Story of His Life* (London, 1936), Edmund Wilson, *To the Finland Station* (Garden City, N.Y., 1940), Robert Payne, *Marx* (New York, 1968), among others.

2. Robert C. Tucker, *Philosophy and Myth in Karl Marx* (London, 1961), Erich Fromm, *Marx's Concept of Man* (New York, 1961),

Notes and References

Gajo Petrovic, *Marx in the Mid-Twentieth Century* (Garden City, N.Y., 1967), and Henry J. Koren, *Marx and the Authentic Man* (Pittsburgh, 1967) are representative of this trend.

3. For a typical example see Lewis S. Feuer, "The Character and Thought of Karl Marx: The Prometheus Complex and Historical Materialism," in *Marx and the Intellectuals: A Set of Post-Ideological Essays* (Garden City, N. Y., 1969), pp. 9–52.

4. Mehring, *Karl Marx*, p. 11.

5. Payne, *Marx*, pp. 61–64.

6. *Ibid.*, pp. 62–63.

7. "Toward the Critique of Hegel's Philosophy of Law: Introduction," in *Writings of the Young Marx*, ed. and trans. Loyd D. Easton and Kurt H. Guddat (Garden City, N.Y., 1967), pp. 263–64.

8. The organizational structure of the *Manuscripts* was undoubtedly affected by Marx's failure to complete them.

9. *Manuscripts* is divided into several sections, the most important of which are on alienated labor, private property and communism, and a critique of the Hegelian philosophy.

10. Of these pages some seventy-five are found in *The German Ideology's* chapter on Feuerbach, in which Marx and Engels for the first time systematically enunciate the principles of historical materialism.

11. Throughout the book this philosophical position and its exponents are sarcastically referred to as "critical criticism," "absolute criticism," or simply "criticism."

12. *The Poverty of Philosophy* (Moscow, n.d.), p. 29.

13. *Herr Vogt* has been included in various versions of Marx and Engels's collected works.

14. Mehring, *Karl Marx*, pp. 296–97.

15. "The Eighteenth Brumaire of Louis Bonaparte," in Karl Marx and Frederick Engels, *Selected Works* (Moscow, 1955), I, 295. Hereafter cited as *Selected Works*.

16. "The Civil War in France," in *Selected Works*, I, 535–36.

17. More than fifteen hundred letters exchanged between them were published in the Collected Works Edition prepared by the Marx-Engels-Lenin Institute in Moscow.

18. In the early 1860s Ferdinand Lassalle emerged as the only socialist leader who had a mass following among Germany's workers. Since he professed to espouse Marx's theories and made repeated attempts to cooperate with him, a public quarrel with Lassalle would have further jeopardized Marx's already rather tenuous ties with the German proletariat.

19. Letter to Engels, July 30, 1862, quoted in Leopold Schwartz-

schild, *Karl Marx: The Red Prussian* (*Karl Marx: Der rote Preusse*) (New York, 1947), p. 277.

20. Letter to Engels, August 15, 1863, in Karl Marx and Frederick Engels, *Selected Correspondence: 1846–1895* (New York, 1942), p. 157. Hereafter cited as *Selected Correspondence*.

21. Letter to Engels, April 2, 1851, in *Selected Correspondence*, p. 36. It is difficult to determine whether this colorful description of economics was merely a reflection of a temporary exasperation with the constant interruptions of Marx's work by never-ending family crises or the expression of an awareness that, previous expectations to the contrary notwithstanding, economics was proving to be not only a dull subject but also something less than the anticipated key to the understanding of all social phenomena.

22. Letter to Engels, August 10, 1869, in *Selected Correspondence*, pp. 261–62. Specifically, this letter expressed Marx's dissatisfaction with what he regarded as Liebknecht's too conciliatory attitude toward Bismarck, but in a more general sense it reflected his growing anger at the former associate's increasingly independent political activities in Germany.

23. Letter to Domela Nieuwenhuis, February 22, 1881, in *Selected Correspondence*, pp. 386–87.

24. The content of Marx's letters can, to some extent, be deduced from his father's replies, many of which have survived.

25. Letter to Ferdinand Lassalle, July 28, 1855, quoted in Mehring's *Karl Marx*, p. 248.

26. Theodor Cuno, "Reminiscences," in *Reminiscences of Marx and Engels* (Moscow, n.d.), p. 210.

27. "Speech at the Anniversary of the *People's Paper*," in *Selected Works*, I, 360.

28. Boris Nicolaievsky and Otto Maenchen-Helfen, *Karl Marx: Man and Fighter* (Philadelphia, 1936), pp. 363–64.

29. For a time during Marx's exile in Great Britain, the payments he received from articles written for the *New York Tribune* constituted his principal source of income.

30. "The North American Civil War," *Die Presse*, October 25, 1861, reprinted in Karl Marx and Frederick Engels, *The Civil War in the United States* (New York, 1961), p. 71.

31. *Capital*, ed. Frederick Engels (New York, 1967), I, 425–27.

32. Letter to Engels, April 2, 1851, in *Selected Correspondence*, p. 36.

33. Letter to Engels, August 5, 1865, in Wilson's *To the Finland Station*, p. 289.

34. *Capital*, I, 132.

35. *Ibid.*, p. 56.

Notes and References

Chapter Eight

1. "Theses on Feuerbach," in *Writings of the Young Marx on Philosophy and Society*, ed. and trans. Loyd D. Easton and Kurt H. Guddat (Garden City, N.Y., 1967), p. 401. Hereafter cited as *Writings of the Young Marx*.

2. "Toward the Critique of Hegel's Philosophy of Law: Introduction," in *Writings of the Young Marx*, p. 259.

3. "Theses on Feuerbach," p. 402.

4. Laura Marx, "Confessions," in *Reminiscences of Marx and Engels* (Moscow, n.d.), p. 266.

5. *Ibid.*

Selected Bibliography

PRIMARY SOURCES

The complete works of Marx and Engels have not yet been translated into English. In 1927 the Marx-Engels-Lenin Institute (Moscow) began the publication of their collected works in German and Russian. The series, published in Germany and edited by D. Rjazanov and V. Adoratskij, was interrupted by Hitler's ascent to power and Stalin's purge of the editors, and was later completed only in Russian. A new German edition, published by the Dietz Verlag (Berlin), was recently finished in East Germany. Both editions suffer from the occasional deletions in the original texts of materials deemed to be embarrassing to the contemporary communist establishments but still constitute an invaluable source of information to all students of Marx.

Writings of the Young Marx on Philosophy and Society. Ed. Loyd D. Easton and Kurt H. Guddat. Garden City, N.Y.: Anchor-Doubleday, 1967. This collection contains Marx's early philosophical essays through *Economic and Philosophic Manuscripts of 1844* and a number of more important articles, letters, and other short pieces written during this period.

The Marx-Engels Reader. Ed. Robert C. Tucker. New York: Norton, 1972. Contains excerpts from their major works translated into excellent English, a rather uncommon accomplishment in this field.

Marx, Karl, and Engels, Frederick. *Selected Works*. 2 vols. Moscow: Foreign Languages Publishing House, 1955. Contains a fairly complete collection of the important shorter works written since 1848.

————. *Selected Correspondence, 1846–1895*. New York: International Publishers, 1942.

————. *Literature and Art: Selections from Their Writings*. New York: International Publishers, 1947.

————. *On Religion*. Moscow: Foreign Languages Publishing House, 1957. Contains excerpts from their works.

————. *The Civil War in the United States*. 3rd ed. New York: International Publishers, 1961. Contains newspaper articles and letters on the American Civil War.

————. *The Holy Family or Critique of Critical Critique.* Moscow: Foreign Languages Publishing House, 1956.

————. *The German Ideology,* Parts 1 and 3. Ed. R. Pascal. New York: International Publishers, 1947.

Marx, Karl. *On Revolution.* Ed. Saul K. Padover. New York: McGraw-Hill, 1971. A valuable collection of Marx's writings on the theory and practice of revolution, including some materials published for the first time in English.

————. *Revolution and Counter-Revolution or Germany in 1848.* Ed. Eleanor Marx-Aveling. Chicago: Charles H. Kerr, n.d. Contains a collection of newspaper articles on the subject.

————. *On Colonialism and Modernization.* Ed. Shlomo Avineri. Garden City, N.Y.: Anchor-Doubleday, 1969.

————. *The Poverty of Philosophy.* Moscow: Foreign Languages Publishing House, n.d.

————. *Pre-Capitalist Economic Formations.* Ed. Eric J. Hobsbawm. New York: International Publishers, 1965. This book includes a section from the manuscript written by Marx in 1857–58 in preparation for his subsequent economic works, *A Contribution to the Critique of Political Economy* and *Capital.* The manuscript was first published in Moscow in 1939–41 under the title of *Fundamentals of the Critique of Political Economy* ("Grundrisse").

————. *A Contribution to the Critique of Political Economy.* Ed. Maurice Dobb. New York: International Publishers, 1970.

————. *Capital.* Ed. Frederick Engels. 3 vols. New York: International Publishers, 1967.

Engels, Frederick. *Anti-Dühring: Herr Eugen Dührings Revolution in Science.* 2nd ed. Moscow: Foreign Languages Publishing House, 1959. Original title: *Herrn Eugen Dührings Umwälzung der Wissenschaft.*

————. *Dialectics of Nature.* Ed. Clemens Dutt. New York: International Publishers, 1940. Original title: *Dialektik der Natur.*

SECONDARY SOURCES

1. Books.

ACTON, HARRY B. *The Illusion of the Epoch.* London: Cohen and West, 1955. A brilliant critique of the theory of historical materialism.

AVINERI, SHLOMO. *The Social and Political Thought of Karl Marx.* Cambridge (England): Cambridge University Press, 1970.

BALZAC, HONORÉ. "The Magic Skin, The Quest for the Absolute and Other Stories." *The Works of Honoré Balzac.* Vol. 1. Philadelphia: Anvil, 1901.

Selected Bibliography

BERLIN, ISAIAH. *Karl Marx: His Life and Environment.* New York: Oxford University Press, 1959. The best short biography in English.

COLE, G. D. H. *The Meaning of Marxism.* Ann Arbor: University of Michigan Press, 1964. A sympathetic interpretation of Marx's doctrine by a leading British socialist.

DEMETZ, PETER. *Marx, Engels, and the Poets.* Chicago: The University of Chicago Press, 1967. A brilliant exposition of Marx's and Engels's literary theory and views. Originally published in German: *Marx, Engels und die Dichter.*

DUPRÉ, LOUIS. *The Philosophical Foundations of Marxism.* New York: Harcourt, Brace, World, 1966. Focuses on Hegel's influence in the development of Marx's thought.

FEUER, LEWIS S. *Marx and the Intellectuals: A Set of Post-Ideological Essays.* New York: Doubleday-Anchor; 1969. Includes an important essay on Marx's Promethean complex.

FROMM, ERICH. *Marx's Concept of Man.* New York: Frederick Ungar, 1961. Somewhat oversimplified interpretation of Marx as a humanist-existentialist philosopher.

GARAUDY, ROGER. *Karl Marx: The Evolution of His Thought.* New York: International Publishers, 1967. An unorthodox interpretation of Marx by a leading French communist intellectual. Original title: *Karl Marx.*

HAMMEN, OSCAR J. *The Red '48ers: Karl Marx and Friedrich Engels.* New York: Scribner's, 1969. A detailed historical analysis of their political actions leading to and during the Revolution of 1848.

HOOK, SIDNEY. *Toward the Understanding of Karl Marx.* New York: John Day, 1933. One of the earlier definitive studies of Marx's thought.

———. *From Hegel to Marx: Studies in the Intellectual Development of Karl Marx.* Ann Arbor: University of Michigan Press, 1962. A penetrating analysis of Hegel's and the Young Hegelians' influence on the development of Marx's philosophy.

KOREN, HENRY J. *Marx and the Authentic Man.* Pittsburgh: Duquesne University Press, 1967. A short introduction to Marx's philosophy, stressing its humanist aspects.

LICHTHEIM, GEORGE. *Marxism: An Historical and Critical Study.* New York: Praeger, 1961. Argues that Marxism was essentially a nineteenth-century phenomenon with marginal impact on the twentieth.

LIFSHITZ, MIKHAIL. *The Philosophy of Art of Karl Marx.* Ed. Angel Flores. New York: Critics Group, 1938. Represents the official Soviet view but is still valuable because there are so few studies on this subject.

MacINTYRE, ALASDAIR. *Marxism and Christianity*. Rev. ed. New York: Schocken, 1968.

MAYER, GUSTAV. *Friedrich Engels*. New York: Knopf, 1936. A standard biography. Original title: *Friedrich Engels*.

MAYO, HENRY B. *Introduction to Marxist Theory*. New York: Oxford University Press, 1960.

McLELLAN, DAVID. *Marx Before Marxism*. New York: Harper Torchbook, 1970. Explores the early, humanist phase in the formation of Marx's thought.

MEHRING, FRANZ. *Karl Marx: The Story of His Life*. London: George Allen and Unwin, 1936. A definitive biography written by a contemporary Marxist. Original title: *Karl Marx: Geschichte seines Lebens*.

NICOLAIEVSKY, BORIS, AND MAENCHEN-HELFEN, OTTO. *Karl Marx: Man and Fighter*. Philadelphia: J. B. Lippincott, 1936. A sympathetic but important biography that contains some information which is lacking in other standard biographies of Marx. Original title: *Karl und Jenny Marx, ein Lebensweg*.

PAYNE, ROBERT. *Marx*. New York: Simon and Schuster, 1968. A refreshing if somewhat unreliable biography that focuses on the "human" side of Marx.

PETROVIC, GAJO. *Marx in the Mid-Twentieth Century*. Garden City, N.Y.: Doubleday-Anchor, 1967. A Yugoslav Marxist's unorthodox interpretation of Marx.

PLAMENATZ, JOHN. *Man and Society*. Vol. 2. New York: McGraw-Hill, 1963. The chapters on Marx contain the most incisive and systematic analysis of his materialist philosophy.

Reminiscences of Marx and Engels. Moscow: Foreign Languages Publishing House, n.d. Contains reminiscences by the members of Marx's family as well as by friends and associates of Marx and Engels.

ROBINSON, JOAN. *Essay on Marxian Economics*. 2nd ed. New York: St. Martin's Press, 1967. A Marxist's critical evaluation of Marx's economic theories.

SCHWARTZSCHILD, LEOPOLD. *Karl Marx: The Red Prussian*. New York: Grosset and Dunlap, 1947. A lively but somewhat unbalanced biography that focuses too much on the authoritarian aspects of Marx's personality. Original title: *Karl Marx: Der Rote Preusse*.

SWEEZY, PAUL M. *The Theory of Capitalist Development*. New York: Monthly Review Press, 1942. A comprehensive analysis of Marx's economic views by an American Marxist.

TUCKER, ROBERT C. *Philosophy and Myth in Karl Marx*. Cambridge (England): Cambridge University Press, 1961. A brilliant pioneering study emphasizing Marx's debt to the concepts of God

Selected Bibliography

and man in German philosophy and the philosophical continuity between his early humanist and subsequent historical-materialist phases.

WILSON, EDMUND. *To the Finland Station.* Garden City, N.Y.: Doubleday-Anchor, 1940. The chapters on Marx include the discussion of the aesthetic aspects of his thought and the literary content of his writings.

2. Articles.

ELVIN, H. L. "Marx and the Marxists as Literary Critics." *Journal of Adult Education,* 10 (1938), 260–76. Deemphasizes the relationship between the production process and the aesthetic elements of the superstructure in Marx's materialist philosophy.

LIFSCHITZ, M. "Marx on Esthetics." *International Literature,* 3 (1933), 75–91. Argues the validity of the "uneven development of art and society" doctrine.

NECHKINA, M. "Shakespeare in Karl Marx's 'Capital.'" *International Literature,* 5 (1935), 75–81. The author claims that Marx's use of Shakespearean quotations reflected his view of the British playwright and his works as representative of a definite stage in the historical process. Thus, M. Nechkina argues that Marx regarded Falstaff as a typical operator in the era of primitive accumulation.

SCHILLER, F. "Marx and Engels on Balzac." *International Literature,* 3 (1933), 113–24. Attempts to explain why Marx's fascination with Balzac did not violate the precepts of historical materialism.

TIMOFYEYEV, L. "Karl Marx on Literature." *International Literature,* 13 (1943), 63–66.

TROSCHENKO, E. "Marx on Literature." *International Literature,* 4 (1934), 138–48. Argues that Marx's views on literature laid the foundations of "socialist realism."

WILSON, EDMUND. "Art, the Proletariat and Marx." *The New Republic,* August 23, 1933, pp. 41–45.

———. "Marxism and Literature." *Atlantic Monthly,* 160 (1937), 741–51.

———. "Herr Vogt." *The New Republic,* November 15, 1939, pp. 106–109.

Index

Index